CAMBRIDGE LIBRARY COLLECTION

Books of enduring scholarly value

Cambridge

The city of Cambridge received its royal charter in 1201, having already been home to Britons, Romans and Anglo-Saxons for many centuries. Cambridge University was founded soon afterwards and celebrates its octocentenary in 2009. This series explores the history and influence of Cambridge as a centre of science, learning, and discovery, its contributions to national and global politics and culture, and its inevitable controversies and scandals.

Introduction to Cambridge

S.C. Roberts, a senior officer of Cambridge University Press as Secretary to the Press Syndicate, wrote several works for Cambridge, including a history of the Press and this handy visitors' guide to the University. After its first publication in 1934, this book went through a number of editions and was thoroughly updated after the Second World War. Roberts introduces the reader to the University from within, covering its history, its finest buildings, the way the University was run and the daily life of the undergraduate. The informal style makes this a highly entertaining introduction to the Cambridge of the 1930s and 40s: the entrance examination, the midnight curfew for undergraduates, the then new University Library, and the systems of governance. For everyone connected with Cambridge, this little book provides fascinating insights into what has and has not changed in the ancient university city since the Second World War.

Cambridge University Press has long been a pioneer in the reissuing of out-of-print titles from its own backlist, producing digital reprints of books that are still sought after by scholars and students but could not be reprinted economically using traditional technology. The Cambridge Library Collection extends this activity to a wider range of books which are still of importance to researchers and professionals, either for the source material they contain, or as landmarks in the history of their academic discipline.

Drawing from the world-renowned collections in the Cambridge University Library, and guided by the advice of experts in each subject area, Cambridge University Press is using state-of-the-art scanning machines in its own Printing House to capture the content of each book selected for inclusion. The files are processed to give a consistently clear, crisp image, and the books finished to the high quality standard for which the Press is recognised around the world. The latest print-on-demand technology ensures that the books will remain available indefinitely, and that orders for single or multiple copies can quickly be supplied.

The Cambridge Library Collection will bring back to life books of enduring scholarly value across a wide range of disciplines in the humanities and social sciences and in science and technology.

Introduction to Cambridge

A Brief Guide to the University from Within

SYDNEY CASTLE ROBERTS

CAMBRIDGE
UNIVERSITY PRESS

CAMBRIDGE UNIVERSITY PRESS

Cambridge New York Melbourne Madrid Cape Town Singapore São Paolo Delhi

Published in the United States of America by Cambridge University Press, New York

www.cambridge.org
Information on this title: www.cambridge.org/9781108003469

This edition first published 1934
This digitally printed version 2009

ISBN 978-1-108-00346-9

This book reproduces the text of the original edition. The content and language reflect
the beliefs, practices and terminology of their time, and have not been updated.

INTRODUCTION TO CAMBRIDGE

INTRODUCTION TO CAMBRIDGE

by

S. C. ROBERTS, M.A.

Fellow of Pembroke College

CAMBRIDGE

at the University Press

1948

Printed in Great Britain at the University Press, Cambridge
(Brooke Crutchley, University Printer)
and published by the Cambridge University Press
(Cambridge, and Bentley House, London)
Agents for U.S.A., Canada, and India: Macmillan

First Edition	1934
Second Edition, revised	1938
Third Edition, revised	1943
Reprinted	1944, 1945
Fourth Edition, revised	1946
Fifth Edition, revised	1948

CONTENTS

ILLUSTRATIONS

PREFACE

This book does not seek to compete with the many topographical guide-books to Cambridge which are already available; still less does it emulate the encyclopaedic quality of *The Student's Handbook*.

It attempts rather to give a simple account of how the University of Cambridge has come, in the course of seven centuries, to be what it is to-day; to present a picture, in outline, of the working of the present academic system, from the points of view both of the don and of the undergraduate; and to show, in particular, the close interdependence of university and college both in teaching and in administration.

I am indebted for valuable help and criticism to Mr Will Spens, Master of Corpus Christi College, to Mr E. Harrison, Registrary of the University, and to Mr D. A. Winstanley, Fellow of Trinity College.

S. C. R.

June 1934

I

PAST AND PRESENT

The official answer to the question "What is the University of Cambridge?" is at once concise and comprehensive. It is "a corporation which, in addition to the usual powers of corporations, such as the ownership of property, possesses the rights of exercising disciplinary authority over its members, returning two representatives to Parliament, and conferring degrees".

Behind this definition lie some 700 years of history. In the twelfth century the word *universitas* signified simply an organised body of men, a corporation. Later it was applied especially to a *universitas scholarium*, a corporation of scholars organised under the direction of "Masters".

The exact date of the first formation of such a body of scholars in Cambridge is uncertain. Early in the twelfth century the canons of St Giles moved from under the castle walls to a priory at Barnwell; a little later was founded the nunnery of St Rhadegund, which afterwards was converted into Jesus College; on the site of St John's College stood a hospital of Augustinian canons; but it is not until the beginning of the next century that we have definite evidence of the existence of bodies of students in Cambridge. In 1209 there was an upheaval in the University of Oxford which led to a migration of a considerable number of scholars to Cambridge; and while it is clear that Oxford may claim seniority of foundation, it may well be argued that there would have been no migration to Cambridge if there had not been schools already in existence on the banks of the Cam. Certainly by the year 1231 the body of Cambridge students was sufficiently important and sufficiently active to cause King Henry III to issue a number of writs for the punishment of disorderly scholars by the Sheriff, for the expulsion of students who were not under the direction of a master, and for the regulation of the rents of lodgings by two masters and two "good and lawful men of the town". These injunctions throw a certain light on the life and conduct of the medieval student. According to one historian, the troubles were provoked by "a crew of pretenders to scholarship" who "lived under no discipline, having no tutor saving him who teacheth all mischief". "Town and gown" riots were a common feature of the Middle Ages—"strifes, fights, spoilings, breaking open of houses, woundings and murder betwixt the burgesses and the scholars of Cambridge, and that in the very Lent, that with the holy time holy persons also might be violated". Nevertheless, the early university had its organisation for teaching. The student entered it at the age of fourteen or earlier, with little knowledge except of elementary Latin. After a preliminary course in Latin

2

grammar, he was set to study Logic during his first year and at the end of it was put to the test of disputation; then followed Rhetoric, which consisted, in effect, of a study of a Latin translation of Aristotle's treatise. Having completed this *trivium*, or threefold course, and having again carried through the prescribed disputation, the student became an "incepting" or "commencing" bachelor and proceeded to the *quadrivium*, or fourfold course of arithmetic, geometry, music, and astronomy. This course occupied four years, at the end of which the student was qualified to become a Master of Arts and to begin to give lectures himself.

As a body, the thirteenth-century university was very loosely held together. The medieval student was essentially a wanderer, and an outbreak of the plague or a violent quarrel with the town might lead to a dispersal of large numbers. Both teachers and pupils lived where they liked, and along what is now Senate-House Passage there was a group of houses (the Grammar School, the Law School, the Arts School, and so on) in which lectures were given. Later the university acquired land and buildings near by, but it was not until the fifteenth century that the "Schools" were concentrated in a quadrangular building which was ultimately absorbed by the old University Library. In the early days of the university lectures were also given at the house founded by the Franciscans on the present site of Sidney Sussex College, and larger gatherings of the university were held in Great St Mary's Church.

Throughout the thirteenth century there were many attempts to improve university discipline, and in 1276 it was laid down that "no one shall receive a scholar who has not had a fixed master within fifteen days after the said scholar has entered the University". This ordinance had the special approval of Hugh de Balsham, Bishop of Ely from 1257 to 1286, and it was due to him that a solution of the university's disciplinary difficulties was found in the inauguration of the college system.

Hugh de Balsham, espousing the cause of the ordinary priest, introduced a body of secular scholars into the Augustinian Hospital of St John. The experiment was a failure and the Bishop was obliged to remove his scholars; the Augustinians on their part surrendered to him St Peter's Church (on the site of which St Mary the Less now stands) and two neighbouring hostels. Thus Peterhouse, the first Cambridge college, came into being, and on 28 May 1284 "the studious scholars who should in everything live together as students in the University of Cambridge according to the rule of the Scholars at Oxford who are called of Merton" were confirmed by Royal Charter in the possession of their *Domus Sancti Petri*. It was not until 1338 that Peterhouse actually received its statutes from Hugh de Balsham's successor. No other college was founded in the thirteenth century, but in 1324 Hervey de Stanton, Chancellor of the Exchequer, established a college of the "scholars of St Michael", a foundation known as Michaelhouse and afterwards merged in Trinity College. Meanwhile the university itself had received full and formal recognition. In 1317 Edward II requested Pope John XXII to confirm the privileges of the university, and in the following year the Pope issued a bull in which it was decreed that Cambridge should be a *studium generale* and that the masters and scholars should enjoy all the rights belonging to a *universitas*; in particular, these rights included that of a doctor of the University of Cambridge to lecture in any part of Christendom; also, the university was made independent of the jurisdiction of the Bishop of the diocese and the supreme power was vested in the head of the university, the Chancellor.[1]

The early part of the fourteenth century was rich in new foundations. In 1326 the university purchased two houses and converted them into a house of learning which was known as University Hall. Twelve years later the building was re-endowed and reconstructed by Elizabeth de Burgh, Countess of Clare, in whose honour it became Clare College. About the same time Edward III established in a college that was known as King's Hall thirty-two scholars who had been maintained by his father. Like Michaelhouse, this foundation was afterwards absorbed by Henry VIII into Trinity College. Pembroke College was founded in 1347 by Mary de Saint Paul, wife of Aymer de Valence, Earl of Pembroke, the foundation consisting of a master, twenty-four fellows, and six scholars, who were enjoined to be constant in their visits to Denny Abbey, a

[1] The earliest mention of a Chancellor is in 1246. Actually the Bishops of Ely for long disputed the independence of the university.

nunnery near Waterbeach founded by the same benefact-
ress. A year later Edmund Gonville, Rector of Terring-
ton in Norfolk, founded a college which came to be known
as Gonville Hall. On Gonville's death in 1351, his design
was completed by William Bateman, Bishop of Norwich,
who moved the scholars from their tenements in what is
now Free School Lane to a site just opposite the college
—Trinity Hall—which he himself had founded in 1350.
Gonville Hall was re-founded by its most famous *alumnus*,
John Caius, in 1557, and its name was changed to Gonville
and Caius College. Meanwhile, in 1352, Corpus Christi
College had been founded by two gilds of the town—the
Gild of Corpus Christi and the Gild of the Blessed Virgin
Mary, who merged their identity in that of the college.

By the end of the fourteenth century the university
itself had become a well-organised and powerful body.
Its government lay in the hands of the Chancellor and two
academic assemblies—the House of Regents, the active
teachers, and the House of Non-Regents, who were resident members in the university not engaged in teaching.
The Non-Regents were not concerned with regulations
for teaching, but, concurrently with the Regents, exercised a measure of control over matters of property and
privilege. The Chancellor, who could depute some of his
duties to a Vice-Chancellor, was elected every two years
by the Regents, and held wide powers. He acted as judge
in his own court to hear cases in which a scholar was concerned. Besides being the administrator of university
discipline, he also had ecclesiastical authority, including

that of excommunication and absolution. This independence was stoutly challenged by the Bishops of Ely. One of them, Thomas Arundel, Bishop of Ely from 1374 to 1388, secured a decision in the ecclesiastical court that the Chancellor should take an oath of canonical obedience. But in 1430 the university successfully laid its case before Pope Martin V and the Chancellor's claim to ecclesiastical jurisdiction exclusive of any archbishop or bishop was recognised and approved.

The Proctors also were officials of great importance in the medieval university. Two were chosen every year by the Regents. They are first mentioned in 1275, and there is a continuous record of their appointment since 1314. They were responsible for the conduct of disputations in the Schools and of university ceremonies; they supervised the markets with a view to the supplies required for the scholars; they were responsible for university finance and for repressing disturbances in the streets.

In the fifteenth century the most notable college foundation was that of King's College, founded in 1441 by Henry VI, who, in his double foundation of Eton and King's, followed the plan of William of Wykeham, founder of Winchester College and New College, Oxford. The scholars of King's were to be drawn only from Eton[1] and were recognised as "exempt from the power, dominion, and jurisdiction of the chancellor, vice-chancellor, proctors, and ministers of the university", so far as all

[1] It was not until 1861 that King's College was thrown open to non-Etonians.

7

disciplinary matters were concerned. Among the many buildings which Henry VI cleared to make room for his famous chapel was God's House, a small college which was removed to a site opposite St Andrew's Church. Other foundations of the fifteenth century were Queens' College, founded in 1448 by Margaret of Anjou, wife of Henry VI, at the instigation of Andrew Doket. When Edward IV came to the throne, his Queen, Elizabeth Woodville, became patroness and co-foundress of the college, which has accordingly been described as the first outward symbol of the reconciliation of York and Lancaster.[1] A smaller foundation was that of St Catharine's College, founded in 1473 by Robert Wodelarke, Provost of King's; and in 1496 John Alcock, Bishop of Ely, finding the nunnery of St Rhadegund in a state of neglect and dilapidation, obtained leave of the King to found a college in its place. This was the beginning of Jesus College.

Up to the end of the fifteenth century it may be said, in general, that theology, canon law, civil law, and medicine were the main subjects to which the student might turn after passing through the "arts" course represented by the *trivium* and *quadrivium*. To obtain a doctorate in one of these subjects, a further residence of at least eight years at the university was necessary. The medieval student derived his instruction partly from formal lectures, partly from classes at which the master propounded questions for discussion, partly from text-books in the college

[1] The association of two queens with the foundation of the college is indicated by the apostrophe—Queens', *not* Queen's.

8

library. All these texts were in Latin, and, after reaching the necessary standard of grammatical competence, the student was chiefly concerned with Aristotle and the scholastic philosophers. There was little or no study of poetry, history, or oratory. But although theology and philosophy were prominent in the curriculum, the medieval colleges were not monastic. The scholars for whom they were founded were prepared for entry into the world of affairs as well as for entry into Holy Orders, and well before the end of the fifteenth century the practice of admitting *pensionarii* or *commensales*, that is, students who paid for their board, lodging, and instruction, was established.[1]

At the beginning of the sixteenth century the most active figure in the university was that of John Fisher, Master of Michaelhouse, and afterwards President of Queens', Vice-Chancellor in 1501 and elected Chancellor for life in 1504. The Lady Margaret, the mother of Henry VII, had appointed him as her confessor, and he was the first holder of the Professorship of Divinity which she founded in 1502.[2] Further, it was through Fisher's influence and advice that the Lady Margaret re-founded

[1] Later, in the eighteenth century, these students came to be divided into two classes—rich and poor. The sons of men of wealth and distinction were entered as "Fellow-Commoners" and dined at the Fellows' table in Hall; poor men's sons, on the other hand, often came up as "Sizars" and were fed on the leavings of the Fellows' table.

[2] This professorship, the oldest in the university, still bears the Lady Margaret's name.

9

God's House, which came to be more commonly known as Christ's College. The foundation was a large one, providing for twelve fellows and forty-seven scholars, and there was also a statutory provision for "pensioners" not on the foundation; a college lecturer was provided to deliver courses on the "works of the poets and orators", a noteworthy sign of the Renaissance spirit. Before her death in 1509, the Lady Margaret had also approved the foundation of a new college in place of the old Hospital of St John, and Fisher was one of the executors entrusted with the completion of the project. The new college, consisting of a master and thirty-one fellows, came into being in 1511.

Fisher was also responsible for introducing to Cambridge the greatest scholar of the Renaissance, Erasmus. Erasmus came to Queens' about 1510 and worked there upon the New Testament and upon his edition of St Jerome. He became Lady Margaret's Professor in 1511 and was the first teacher of Greek in Cambridge. His audiences were small, but the seed of the critical spirit had been sown, and one of his pupils, Richard Croke, came back, after spending some time on the continent, to continue the teaching of Greek in Cambridge in 1519. Erasmus was probably responsible also for the introduction of printing into Cambridge. Certainly John Siberch, who, with the approval of the University, set up a printing-press in 1521, was a friend of his, and one of the books printed by him was Erasmus' own treatise *De Conscribendis Epistolis*. Later, in 1534, the university received a charter from Henry VIII authorising the appointment of printers who should print all manner of books subject to the approval of the Chancellor, and from the sixteenth century to the present day the office of university printer has been filled without interruption. Meanwhile the Reformation movement was making itself felt in Cambridge. Thomas Bilney, inspired by Erasmus' exposition of the New Testament, and Hugh Latimer, who preached in St Edward's Church his famous Sermons on the Card, were prominent leaders of the movement, and the whole university was divided into strongly opposed parties when the question of the legality of Henry VIII's marriage to Catherine of Aragon was referred to the university. Fisher was put to death in 1535 for refusing to accept the King's supremacy and was succeeded as Chancellor by Thomas Cromwell, who immediately issued a series of Royal Injunctions which demanded full acceptance of the royal supremacy; they also enjoined that lectures on the canon law should be abolished; that daily lectures on Latin and Greek should be given in each college; and that the texts of the scholastic philosophers should give place to the new learning which was growing round the Old and New Testaments.

The dissolution of the monasteries meant, of course, the destruction of the various religious houses in Cambridge, and, although the standard of scholarship was rising under the influence of Roger Ascham, John Cheke and others, there was a serious decline in the total number of students. However, so far as the university was con-

cerned, Henry VIII made amends. In 1540 he founded
Regius Professorships in Divinity, Civil Law, Physic,
Hebrew, and Greek. The first Professor of Civil Law was
Thomas Smith, and it was when he was Vice-Chancellor
in 1544 that a statute was passed by which the student was
required to present himself to the Registrary of the University[1] for matriculation. Amongst the religious houses
which were dissolved at this time was Buckingham College, a hostel for Benedictine monks; in 1542 it was re-
founded, as Magdalene College, by Thomas Lord Audley
of Walden, to whom it had been granted by the King for
that purpose. An Act for the Dissolution of Colleges
passed in 1545 caused grave alarm in Cambridge. It gave
the King power to appoint commissioners to report upon
the condition of colleges and similar foundations. Cambridge was fortunate in having Matthew Parker, Master
of Corpus and Vice-Chancellor of the University, John
Redman, afterwards Master of Trinity, and William Mey,
President of Queens', as its commissioners, and their report to the King showed with careful emphasis that the
expenditure of each college was in excess of its income.
The university also addressed a letter to Queen Catherine
(Parr), begging that she would influence the King on the
university's behalf, and received a favourable reply to the
effect that His Majesty was such a patron to good learning
that he would rather advance learning and erect new occasion thereof than confound the ancient and godly institutions of Cambridge. Certainly in the following year

[1] This office had been established in 1506.

Henry VIII erected a new occasion of learning in the foundation of Trinity College, a college of "literature, the sciences, philosophy, good arts, and sacred theology", which was to occupy the "soil, ground, sites, and precincts" of King's Hall, Michaelhouse and other hostels, and was to have a master and sixty fellows and scholars. Trinity remains the largest of college foundations, and it has been described as the most striking example of the change from the medieval to the modern conception of education and learning. In the stormy reign of Mary, in the course of which Cranmer, Latimer, and Ridley were burnt at Oxford and John Hullyer, of King's, suffered a like fate on Jesus Green at Cambridge, the most important event in college history was the re-founding of Gonville Hall by John Caius in 1557.

By the time of Elizabeth, Cambridge had come to be recognised as a stronghold of the Reformed Church of England, and the main controversies lay between Anglicans and Puritans. New statutes for the university were approved by the Queen in 1570 and effected important changes in the methods of university government. In particular, the heads of colleges became "a distinct and separate estate in the government of the University": they were empowered to nominate two candidates for the Vice-Chancellorship, the final choice being made by the Regents and Non-Regents acting together; they were also given an important share in the choice of the *caput senatus*, which is first mentioned in 1526 as a body to advise the Chancellor and, in particular, to approve

13

Graces for submission to the Senate.[1] The statutes of 1570 laid down that this *Caput*, consisting of the Chancellor, three Doctors, and two Masters of Arts, should be appointed at the beginning of the academical year and should remain in office until the end of it. The ancient powers of the Proctors were at the same time curtailed. Though still formally elected by the Regents, they were to be nominated by the colleges in rotation—a method which has prevailed to the present day; their control of university finance was transferred to the Chancellor; they ceased to be the chief representatives of the House of Regents and their authority was made subordinate to that of the Chancellor. The main effect of the Elizabethan statutes was to concentrate power in the hands of the Vice-Chancellor and the Heads of Houses, and the university lived under the constitution of 1570 for nearly three hundred years. In 1573 it received its grant of arms: *gules a cross ermine and four gold leopards with a book gules upon the cross.*

Two colleges founded in the later part of the sixteenth century may be taken as representing the more moderate Puritanism of the period—Emmanuel, founded by Sir Walter Mildmay on the site of a Dominican house in 1584, and Sidney Sussex, founded by Lady Frances (daughter of Sir William Sidney and widow of the second Earl of Sussex) in 1596.

It was at the beginning of the reign of James I that the

[1] The Council of the Senate performs the same function to-day. See p. 55.

University of Cambridge, like that of Oxford, received the right, which it still holds, of returning two members to Parliament, their special duty being to keep Parliament informed "of the true state of the university and of every particular college". Both Elizabeth and James I visited Cambridge and witnessed performances of college plays. *Ignoramus*, produced in Clare College for James I in 1615, was a satirical attack upon the profession of the Common Law and gave the King such pleasure that he returned to Cambridge to see it a second time.[1]

During the Civil War the townsmen of Cambridge were, as a whole, on the Parliamentary side; the colleges, on the other hand, were Royalist and sent contributions to the King's defence. Three heads of colleges were imprisoned by Cromwell for conveying college plate to the King's headquarters, and in 1643 a Parliamentary garrison was established in the town. College bridges were removed and "superstitious images and pictures" in college chapels destroyed. In the next year those members of the university (including most of the heads of colleges) who refused to accept the Solemn League and Covenant were expelled from their offices. In 1660 they returned, and the Act of Uniformity ensured that all holders of university and college offices should declare armed resistance to the Crown unlawful and should conform to the liturgy of the Church of England.

One of the features of the intellectual life of Restoration

---

[1] These plays were disliked by the Puritans and were censured by Milton in his *Apology for Smectymnuus*.

Cambridge was the great attention paid to the study of Plato, as contrasted with the medieval devotion to Aristotle and the Schoolmen. A group of scholars including Whichcote, John Smith, Cudworth and Henry More came to be known as the Cambridge Platonists and aimed at a reconciliation of the claims of revealed religion and metaphysical philosophy. About the same time Cambridge began for the first time to pay serious attention to mathematics. The arithmetic, geometry, and astronomy of the medieval *quadrivium* were associated with such subjects as the cosmography of Pliny, the mystical properties of numbers as expounded by Pythagoras, and various astrological enquiries; in the curriculum laid down by the Elizabethan statutes there was no mention of mathematics, and John Wallis, of Emmanuel, migrated to Oxford in 1649 since at Cambridge "mathematics were scarce looked upon as academical studies". At Oxford Professorships of Geometry and Astronomy had been established since 1619, but at Cambridge the first Chair of Mathematics (the Lucasian) was not founded until 1663. Its first holder was Isaac Barrow and its second Isaac Newton, who was appointed in 1669. In the succeeding twenty years the state of mathematical knowledge was completely transformed, and since the publication of Newton's *Principia* in 1687 the mathematical fame of Cambridge has been securely established. In the early years of the eighteenth century Professorships of Modern History and Astronomy were founded.

The most vigorous Cambridge personality of the

period was that of Richard Bentley, who was installed as Master of Trinity in 1700. Prominent himself as a classical scholar, he was engaged for many years in violent dissensions with the fellows of his own college. His activity in the promotion of scholarship in various departments of the university was remarkable: he encouraged Newton to publish a second edition of his *Principia*; he built an observatory over the Great Gate of Trinity for Roger Cotes, the first Professor of Astronomy; he reorganised the University Press. From a small work compiled by Daniel Waterland, Master of Magdalene, in 1706 and entitled *Advice to a Young Student*, we may gain some idea of the undergraduate curriculum at this period. The work is divided under three heads: philosophical, classical, and religious. Under the first the student proceeds from Euclid's *Elements* to Whiston's *Astronomy*, Locke's *Human Understanding*, and Newton's *Opticks*; under the second from Terence and Xenophon to Cicero, Homer, Virgil, Sophocles, Juvenal, and so on; under the third, *Sermons* are prominent and are supplemented by such works as Grotius, *de Veritate Religionis Christianæ* and Pearson, *On the Creed*. In particular, the student is advised to devote his mornings and evenings to philosophy, and his afternoons to classics "as requiring less coolness"; in general, for the sake of peace and order to bear with some little rudeness and some imperious carriage from his seniors in college.

To this period belongs the building which for two hundred years has come to be the centre of university ceremony and university legislation—the Senate-House, designed by James Gibbs and completed in 1730. With the Senate-House is associated the Tripos, the name given to a Cambridge Honours examination. The first Tripos list belongs to the year 1747–8, but as early as 1498 there are records of an *Ordo Senioritatis*, that is, an order of academic seniority of those who had passed through the *trivium* to the degree of Bachelor of Arts. It was not until the eighteenth century that this order became an order of merit. In the Middle Ages the candidate had been put to the test in his third year, when he was required to dispute in the Schools (twice in defence of his own thesis and twice in attack upon others[1]) upon questions of scholastic philosophy propounded by the Proctors.

From the time of the Elizabethan statutes onwards the schoolmen gave place to more modern philosophers and the curriculum was further modified by the rapid rise to prominence of mathematics. But though the subjects changed, the procedure was little altered. The eighteenth-century undergraduate performed his acts and opponencies and was also submitted to an oral examination. After answering a formal question in the Schools, he became a "determiner" and, on the Thursday after mid-Lent Sunday was pronounced by the Proctor to be a full Bachelor of Arts.

From the time of the fifteenth century an "ould

[1] These were known as "Acts" and "Opponencies" respectively.

18

CAMBRIDGE FROM THE AIR

Phot. Aerofilms

ADMISSION OF THE SENIOR WRANGLER, 1842

R. B. Harraden

bachelour" had sat in front of the Proctors to argue with the candidate; he sat on a three-legged stool and was known as "Mr Tripos" and his speeches (or verses in Latin relating to the subject of discussion) came to be known as "Tripos verses". "Mr Tripos" was given to satire and frivolity in the composition of these verses and, after the disappearance of "Mr Tripos" himself, the tradition of his verses was preserved. In 1747–8 the custom was begun of printing the list of successful candidates on the back of the sheets of Tripos verses. The lists, divided into (1) Wranglers and Senior Optimes, (2) Junior Optimes, (3) οἱ πολλοί, or Poll Men,[1] came to be known as "the Tripos", and eventually the term was applied to the examination itself.

It was in the eighteenth century that the examination of candidates gradually assumed a greater importance than the exercises performed by them in disputation; and from 1763 onwards the exercises, though not abolished until 1839, were used only as a means of preliminary classification. It was on the results of the examination, held in the Senate-House, that the order of names in the Tripos list was compiled. Written answers were first required about 1772, but printed examination papers were not introduced until 1827. Meanwhile the Woodwardian Professorship of Geology and the Lowndean

---

[1] Wrangler, Senior Optime, and Junior Optime survive as the designation of a candidate who attains the first, second, or third class in Part II of the Mathematical Tripos. The term "Poll Man" is still applied to a man who takes a pass degree (see p. 77).

Professorship of Astronomy and Geometry had been founded, but it was not until the nineteenth century that formal examinations for degrees in subjects other than mathematics were established.

The opening of the nineteenth century saw the foundation of a new college. Founded under the will of Sir George Downing, Bart., who died in 1749, Downing College obtained a royal charter in 1800, the foundation including a Professor of the Laws of England and a Professor of Medicine.

The story of the university in the nineteenth century is a story of emancipation, expansion, and elaboration. Reforms were prominent in the public mind, and gradually the university was brought under their influence. Up to 1871 no Dissenter could proceed to the degree of M.A. or hold a college fellowship. In 1834 a number of resident graduates presented a petition to the House of Commons for the abolition of all religious tests: a Bill embodying this recommendation was passed through the House of Commons, but was thrown out by the House of Lords, and it was not until 1871 that religious tests were finally abolished, both in the university and in the colleges.[1] Meanwhile reformers had turned their attention to the curriculum. In 1824 the Classical Tripos was founded,

[1] Selwyn College (see p. 24) requires that its members shall belong to the Church of England or to a Church in communion therewith. Originally a "Public Hostel", it became by the University Statutes of 1926 an "Approved Foundation" in the university.

but no candidate was allowed to sit for the examination unless he had previously obtained at least third class honours in mathematics—a condition which was maintained until 1850. After this emancipation, one subject after another secured its Tripos: the first lists of Moral Sciences and Natural Sciences appeared in 1851; of Law in 1859; of History in 1870. Two Royal Commissions enquired into the state of the university in the nineteenth century: the first was appointed in 1850 and proposed "the restoration in its integrity of the ancient supervision of the university over the studies of its members". To this end it recommended the opening of "avenues for acquiring academical honours in many new and distinct branches of knowledge", the removal of restrictions upon elections to fellowships and scholarships, and the desirability of the colleges contributing towards the cost of university teaching. Changes in the University and College Statutes followed in due course, and in 1856 a Council of the Senate was constituted to take the place of the old *Caput*; but a demand for a wider measure of reform led to the appointment of another Royal Commission in 1872, and ten years later the Universities of Oxford and Cambridge Act was approved by the Queen in Council. One of the most notable changes effected by this Act was the provision that a married man might retain his fellowship of a college. Up to this time a fellow of a college who decided to marry had been obliged to forfeit his fellowship, and the new dispensation made a profound alteration in the social life of the university. Further,

21

tenure of a fellowship for life was to be dependent on the association of the fellowship with some office in the college or university, and provision was made for inter-collegiate teaching. The changes inaugurated by these statutes of 1882 were fundamental; the eighteenth-century fellow of a college, if he remained unmarried, was secure for life within the walls of his college, whether he played any active part in teaching or not; he was commonly in orders, and if he married, would normally become the holder of one of the livings in the gift of his college. If he were a scholar of distinction, he might attain to a professorship; and while Cambridge in the eighteenth century produced some notable scholars—Bentley and Porson among them —election to a professorship did not necessarily imply a profound knowledge of the subject in question. Richard Watson, for instance, who was appointed Professor of Chemistry in 1764, declared that at the time "he knew nothing at all of chemistry, had never read a syllable on the subject, nor seen a single experiment in it". He had little more knowledge of theology when he became Professor of Divinity in 1771.

To an example of this kind the state of learning and research in Cambridge a hundred years later presents a striking contrast. Each of the main subjects has its Tripos, and names such as those of Lightfoot, Westcott, Hort, Jebb, Sidgwick, Stokes, Seeley, and Clerk Maxwell suggest the new standard that had been reached in professorial elections. In particular, the establishment of the Cavendish Laboratory of Experimental Physics in 1871 with Clerk Maxwell at its head led to a pre-eminence in the world of experimental physics which Cambridge still holds.

It was in the middle of the nineteenth century that two movements were inaugurated to bring the university into closer relations with education outside its own walls. The first of these was the establishment of "Local Examinations", that is, of examinations of boys and girls at school, conducted under the auspices of the university and held at various centres throughout the country. In 1858, the first year in which Local Examinations were held, 370 candidates were examined. To-day there are centres all over the British Empire, and the total number of candidates in 1942 was over 24,500. Three grades of examination are annually held: on the results of the Higher School Certificate examination State Scholarships are awarded by the Board of Education; on the results of the School Certificate examination a large number of candidates qualify for matriculation at the university.[1] A similar series of examinations in schools has since 1873 been conducted by an Oxford and Cambridge Schools Examination Board, on which both universities are represented.

The other movement was the University Extension Movement, which grew out of lectures given in the nórth of England by James Stuart, Fellow of Trinity, in 1867 and 1868. Local (or "Extension") lectures were first arranged under the auspices of the university in

[1] See p. 72.

1872, and the Board of Extra-Mural Studies now or-
ganises courses of lectures throughout the country,
tutorial classes (generally arranged in co-operation with
the Workers' Educational Association), and summer
schools, which are held in Cambridge in the Long
Vacation.

About the same time the claims of women to a share
in university education were first heard. What is now
Girton College was started, through the efforts of Miss
Emily Davies, in a house at Hitchin, with five students,
in 1869. About the same time Henry Sidgwick arranged
lectures for a similar number of students in Cambridge,
and these students moved to what is now the oldest hall
of Newnham College in 1875. Two years before, the first
buildings of Girton College had been erected on the
Huntingdon Road. At first, the women's lectures were
carried on separately, but in 1881 the Tripos examinations were opened to women. Their names were printed
in the lists, but they had no place in the constitution
of the university and degrees were not awarded to
them.

A new college within the university was also founded
about this time—Selwyn College, founded in 1882 in
memory of George Augustus Selwyn and designed for
those "willing to live economically" in a college
"wherein sober living and high culture of the mind may
be combined with Christian training, based upon the
principles of the Church of England".

Earlier, in 1869, the university had made provision for

admitting a certain number of students as "non-collegi-ate", that is, without being attached to a college. The admission and control of such students was in the hands of a university board, who appointed a Censor, and in 1892 Fitzwilliam Hall (afterwards called Fitzwilliam House) became the headquarters of the "non-collegiate" community, and has in fact acquired many of the features of corporate life associated with a college.

Concurrently with the expansion of organised learning in the nineteenth century, there was a large increase in the number of undergraduates. In 1862 there were 1526 in residence; in 1886 there were 2979; in 1914 there were 3676. For the next four years, Cambridge, like other places, was completely transformed. Though the con-tinuity of academical life was never actually broken, only a handful of undergraduates remained. Nearly 14,000 members, past and present, of the university served in the forces of the Crown; of these over 2000 were killed and nearly 3000 wounded. The colleges were put to strange uses: they became barracks, hospitals, staff colleges, headquarters of cadet battalions; khaki was recognised as academical dress and war service as part qualification for a university degree; elderly professors became recruiting officers, special constables, postal censors.

After the Armistice the university was refilled not only with freshmen from the schools, but with demobilised soldiers. The life of the university and of the colleges was quickly reorganised, but a number of problems arose: in particular, the claim of women to full membership of the university which had been rejected in 1897 was strongly pressed. The claim was not admitted, but in 1921 a compromise was reached and a statute in the following year empowered the university to grant titles of degrees to duly qualified members of the two women's colleges; women were not to be matriculated members of the university, but they were entitled to hold professorships and other teaching posts and to be members of Faculties and Faculty Boards. Such was the position until 1947.

Another urgent problem was that of finance. The endowments of the university and of the colleges had not kept pace with the rapid expansion of educational work within the university, and, in particular, the newly developed branches of physical and biological science demanded a greater outlay than the university could itself afford.[1] A Royal Commission on Oxford and Cambridge Universities was set up in 1919 and its report, published in 1922, was followed by the appointment of a Statutory Commission in 1923. The main body of the Commissioners' Statutes was approved by the King in Council in 1926 and it is by these Statutes, supplemented by further Statutes of 1927 and 1928, that the university is now governed.

For more than 20 years the university has received

[1] The first Treasury grant to the University was an annual one of £5873 received in 1914 for the Medical School, and afterwards raised to £8500.

an annual grant from the Treasury and for 1947–48 the total amount, including grants for agricultural and medical education and for new developments in other studies, was £600,500. Under the new statutes the power of legislation is virtually confined to the Regents, that is, to those Masters of Arts and holders of higher degrees who are engaged in teaching and administration in Cambridge; the teaching faculties of the university are more precisely organised, and, although the personal instruction of an undergraduate in college by college teachers still continues, almost all lecturing is now, in practice, university lecturing; provision is also made by the Statutes of 1926 for pensions for all university and college officials.[1]

But it would be a mistake to suppose that the State has been the university's only benefactor in recent years. Many new professorships have been founded and many new laboratories have been built as the result of private benefaction and a munificent grant from the Rockefeller Foundation (International Education Board) helped the university not only to complete its scheme for the extension of various scientific departments, but to build the new University Library. With the transference of the university's books (more than a million and a quarter in number) to this new building, the old "Schools" of the medieval university, round which the old library was

[1] The retiring age for a university or college official is 65; for a master of a college, 70, though some colleges have power to extend their master's tenure of office to the age of 75.

built, have again become the administrative centre of the university.

In 1939 the normal life of Cambridge was again violently interrupted. The exodus of undergraduates was less sudden than in 1914 and, by government order, students of medicine, physics, engineering and some other subjects remained at their work. But the colleges were quickly called upon to house civil servants, R.A.F. cadets, and many other strangers, including the members of several colleges of the University of London. Cambridge became the official headquarters, for purposes of Civil Defence, of the Eastern Region of England, and a well-known Master of a College was appointed Regional Commissioner; air-raid shelters appeared in college courts and "static water" in college gardens; university buildings, like other buildings, had their squads of fire-watchers. Cambridge had an early taste of air-raids, the first bombs being dropped in June 1940; but the colleges escaped damage and the only university building which seriously suffered was the Union Society.[1]

At the end of the war Cambridge was again refilled, and more than refilled, with demobilised men and women from the forces. Many fresh problems arose, especially in relation to their accommodation; but one old problem was solved. In 1947 the university agreed to admit women to full membership.

[1] See page 45.

II

PERAMBULATION

The history of the university may be studied, as may be inferred from the previous chapter, in documents. It may also be studied in wood and brick and stone.

The university is older than the oldest college, but one result of the college system is that the stranger will look in vain for a building called "the University". Until the nineteenth century, indeed, he would have found but two university buildings—the Library and the Senate-House; and the heart of the medieval university must be sought in what was, until 1934, the Catalogue Room of the old University Library and is now again known as the Regent House. This room, built over the old Divinity School at the end of the fourteenth century, served as the Chapel and Senate-House of the university; after the Reformation it was no longer used as a chapel, but remained as the centre of university legislation. The fourteenth-century roof remains, but is hidden by a richly plastered ceiling of 1600. The old Divinity School beneath it, originally built in the middle of the fourteenth century, is the oldest link with university teaching in the Middle Ages.[1] Here lectures and disputations were held, and the schools of Canon Law, built a little later, contributed to form a "Schools" quadrangle.

[1] The earliest record of the university owning land relates to the plot of ground given to it by Nigel de Thornton in 1278. It is included in the western portion of the old library site.

So the "Schools" remained until in the eighteenth and nineteenth centuries they were gradually absorbed into the University Library. Large additions were also made to the library buildings, but not large enough to keep pace with the growth in the number of books. The University Library, possessing books which were bequeathed to the university in 1415, may claim to be the oldest public library in the world. Apart from private benefactions (such as the gift by George I of Bishop Moore's 30,000 volumes in 1715[1] or Lord Acton's 60,000 volumes given by Lord Morley in 1902) the library has the right to claim a copy of every book published in England. This privilege alone involves an accession of about 14,000 books every year.[2] For the housing of a million and a quarter of printed books, more than 10,000 manuscripts and 140,000 maps, the library for many years was in urgent need of a larger building, and the problem was eventually solved by the building of an entirely new library on the ground behind the new Clare building. The old library has now been converted in part into rooms for professors and university officials and so, as has already been noted, once more fulfils its medieval purpose.

With this brief glance at the history of the oldest of university buildings, we may turn to the colleges, and while it is simpler to follow a topographical than a

[1] Still known as the Royal Library and preserved in their eighteenth-century bookcases.

[2] This right was first granted in 1665, but it was not until much later that the university regularly exercised its privilege.

THE UNIVERSITY LIBRARY
(Part of the Royal Library)

PEMBROKE COLLEGE IN THE SEVENTEENTH CENTURY   D. Loggan

chronological order, it is doubly convenient to begin with Peterhouse: it is the oldest foundation and it is the first college the traveller sees if he enters Cambridge by the Trumpington Road. Of the "handsome hall" built with money left to his scholars by Hugh de Balsham, little remains except portions of the doorways; the windows on the south side belong to the fifteenth century and the stained glass, seen both in the hall and in the combination room, is the work of William Morris. Peterhouse, like other early colleges, had at first no chapel of its own, but used St Peter's Church, afterwards rebuilt as St Mary the Less, until 1632. In that year the chapel of Peterhouse was consecrated by Matthew Wren, Master of the College and Bishop of Ely, who "built great Part of the College from the Ground, rescued their Writings and ancient Records from Dust and Worms, and by indefatigable Industry digested them into a good Method and Order". The chapel, which shows a characteristic fusion of Gothic tracery and Classic moulding, is connected with the court on either side by galleries with arcades beneath; in the side windows is some curious Munich glass of the nineteenth century. The master's lodging at Peterhouse was originally above the present combination room, but in 1725 Dr Charles Beaumont, son of a former master, bequeathed to the college his own spacious house on the other side of the road. This house remains the master's lodge and is now flanked by a new block of college buildings. At the north-west corner of the college site is a yet more recent building—and in a more recent style of architecture.

On the north side of the main court is a set of rooms in which Thomas Gray was living early in 1756. Outside the window an iron bar may still be seen. It is the bar which Gray had fixed so that he might hang his rope-ladder on it in case of fire. Two lively members of Peterhouse, knowing Gray's fears, raised a false alarm; Gray slid down the rope and, according to the common story, found himself in a tub of cold water.

Pembroke College, to which Gray migrated after his ill-treatment at Peterhouse, stands on the opposite side of the road. The original college of the foundress was just half the size of the present Old Court. In its early form this court contained "all the component parts of a complete collegiate establishment"—master's lodging, scholars' rooms, chapel, kitchen, hall. In the seventeenth century a new chapel was built to the south and two ranges of chambers[1] on the east. In this form the college remained until 1874, when a misguided deference to architectural opinion induced a bare majority of the fellows to sanction the destruction of the hall, the master's lodge, and the south side of the Old Court. A new hall, master's lodge, and library were built in the neo-Gothic fashion of the time, and other large additions to the college fabric were made in the last century and in this; the latest change being the transformation of the master's lodge of 1874 into college rooms and the

[1] These combined to form a three-sided court still known as Ivy Court, though the ivy has wisely been stripped from the seventeenth-century brickwork.

building of a new lodge in a corner of the college garden.

For chapel the scholars of Pembroke first used the neighbouring church of St Botolph. In 1355 a papal licence was obtained for the building of a college chapel—the first to be built in Cambridge. This chapel was in use for three hundred years. After the Restoration, Matthew Wren, who had been an undergraduate at Pembroke and was imprisoned in the Tower during the Civil War, built his college a new chapel as a thank-offering for his release. The architect was his nephew, and Sir Christopher Wren's first work is seen in Pembroke Chapel. A cloister was also built to link it with the college. The old chapel became a library, and its finely plastered ceiling of 1690 was fortunately saved from the Gothic attacks of the eighteen-seventies.

Gray was not the first poet to live in Pembroke. Edmund Spenser entered the college in 1569, and later came Crashaw, William Mason (Gray's friend), and the unfortunate Christopher Smart. Perhaps the most famous set of rooms in Pembroke is that on the south side of Ivy Court in which Gray and the younger Pitt lived successively in the eighteenth century.

William Pitt came up at the age of fourteen, "too young", as his father hoped, "for the irregularities of a man" but old enough not to "prove troublesome by the Puerile sallies of a Boy". In later years he was a Member of Parliament for the university, and out of the surplus of a fund raised after his death for the erection of a statue in

London, there was built the Pitt Press, nearly opposite his own college. The Pitt Press was an addition to a printing-house which had been in existence for some hundreds of years. The early printers appointed under the Charter of 1534[1] had been printers and booksellers licensed by the university. They had printed some famous books (including the first edition of *Lycidas*), but it was not until the end of the seventeenth century that the Press was organised by Bentley as a university department controlled by a university syndicate. Since 1698 the University Press has continued to be governed by such a syndicate and is wholly the property of the university. It shares with the Oxford University Press and with the King's Printers the privilege of printing the Authorised Version of the Bible and the Prayer Book of 1662. This privilege has been continuously exercised, and during the last sixty years the Press has not only widened its printing activities but has developed a large publishing business. Behind the Pitt Press building is a series of composing-rooms, machine-rooms, offices and ware-houses. Here such books as are accepted by the Syndics of the Press for publication with the imprimatur of the university are set up and printed; when the printed sheets are complete, they are sent to the London publishing house of the Press (Bentley House) to be bound, advertised, and sold to booksellers all over the world.

The University Press occupies nearly the whole of the land between the Pitt Press building and the river Cam.

[1] See p. 11.

On the south side is Mill Lane, which leads to the site of
the ancient King's and Bishop's Mills; in Mill Lane are
the headquarters of the Local Examinations Syndicate
and of the Board of Extra-Mural Studies (Stuart House).
On the north is Silver Street, which leads to Queens'
College. The road in which the college stands is now
called Queens' Lane, but originally it was part of Milne
Street, the main highway of the town before Henry VI
blocked it in order to clear a site for King's College.

The first court of Queens' College illustrates the development of college planning in the fifteenth century;
following the arrangement of a country mansion, it contained rooms, kitchen, butteries, hall, master's lodging,
library, and chapel. It was built in deep-red brick with a
turret at each corner and a noble entrance gateway. The
south turret rooms in the south-west were, according to
tradition, occupied by Erasmus during his sojourn in
Cambridge early in the sixteenth century.[1] The building
of the second, or Cloister Court, was begun about 1460,
and the court is one of the most beautiful of which
Cambridge can boast. Cloisters, built in brick, run round
three sides of it; on the north side is the gallery of the
President's[2] Lodge, built on beams laid across the cloister
walls and since 1911 displaying its beautiful half-timber
work, which for many years had been obscured by plaster.

Queens', like other colleges, has converted its original

[1] See p. 10.
[2] The Head of Queens' College is called the President; of
King's College, the Provost; all the other colleges have a Master.

chapel to other purposes and has a new chapel (completed in 1891) as well as other new buildings on the north side of the college site. From the Cloister Court a wooden bridge, built in 1749, leads to the college grove on the other side of the river, from which the view of the Queens' river-front can be properly appreciated. Flanking the grove an imposing block of buildings was erected in 1936.

Opposite the main building of Queens' is what was once the entrance gateway of St Catharine's College, which was also built to face Milne Street, the fourth side of the court being left open. The present buildings belong for the most part to the seventeenth and eighteenth centuries, and immediately opposite the open court is Corpus Christi College, in which the architecture of the Middle Ages and that of the early nineteenth century can be studied side by side. The Old Court, in spite of certain alterations, is the oldest complete court in Cambridge. The old hall has been converted into a kitchen and the old master's lodging has been adapted to make sets of rooms. But, as a whole, the court remains as one of the best illustrations of the structural character of a medieval college. The New Court, through which the college is entered from Trumpington Street, was built by William Wilkins in 1826. It contains a hall, a library, a master's lodge, and a chapel, as well as sets of rooms. The chapel replaced a sixteenth-century building. In earlier days the college had used the parish church of St Benedict, commonly known as St Bene't's. St Bene't's, whose Saxon tower still stands, is the oldest building in

Cambridge and is still connected with the college by a gallery. The library of Corpus is one of the most famous in the university and in the world, being founded on the collection of Matthew Parker, Archbishop of Canterbury and Master of the College in the sixteenth century.

On the other side of Trumpington Street (which has now become King's Parade) is King's College, dominated both in aspect and in the popular imagination by its famous chapel. Henry VI began the building of his college in 1441. The site first chosen was behind the University Schools. The King himself laid the foundation-stone of the entrance gateway and the building of a court was begun; before it was completed the provost and fellows complained that it was too small. Accordingly the King secured a much more spacious site and the building of the great chapel was begun in 1446. Meanwhile, the original court was partially completed and, as Henry VI was not able to carry out his plans on the larger site, the building behind the old Schools was, in fact, in use until the nineteenth century. In 1828 the old site was sold to the university and a considerable portion of the building was destroyed. To-day the only remnant of the original King's College is to be seen in the western entrance-gate (repaired and restored, but still magnificent) of the Old Schools.

Henry VI prescribed very precisely the form which the chapel of his college was to take: its length was to be 288 feet, its width 40 feet, and its height 90 feet; and the building of the college was to be "clene and substancial, settyng a parte superfluite to too gret curious werkes of entaille and besy moldyng". But the King did not live even to complete his chapel. Parts of it were in use in 1470, but the stonework was not finished until 1515, and shortly afterwards the windows were filled with "the finest series in the world of pictures in glass on a large scale". The stalls and the screen were the gift of Henry VIII, and the arms and initials of Anne Boleyn may be seen in various places on the screen and rood-loft.

It was not until the eighteenth century that the first buildings, other than the chapel, began to appear on the site that Henry VI had secured and cleared. A new court was planned with the chapel as its north side, but only one block was actually built. This is the "Fellows' Building" built by James Gibbs in 1723 with a central archway of surpassing dignity. Over this archway in the later part of the century lived Charles Simeon, and the name "The Saint's Rest" still clings to the rooms he occupied. A hundred years later, when the original court was abandoned, the Gothic Revival had begun, and it is to this period that the stone screen along the street front, the hall, and the library of King's College belong. They were built by Wilkins, the architect of the New Court of Corpus, between 1824 and 1828.

Just to the north of the great west door of the chapel of King's is a gate leading out of the college domain: on the right is the old University Library; on the left is Clare College. Its old court, rebuilt at intervals between 1636 and 1715, has been well described as "more like a palace than a college", and there are few better examples of

THE BACKS AT CLARE COLLEGE

Phot. Hills & Saunders

THE UNIVERSITY LIBRARY

Renaissance work in Cambridge. If some last enchant-
ment of the Middle Ages be sought, it may be found in
the fan-vaulting of the roof of the entrance gateway.
Beyond the court is an equally harmonious bridge, built
by Thomas Grumbold, master-mason, in 1640. The
bridge leads over the river to an avenue of limes, and the
avenue leads to Queens' Road, the road that runs along
the "Backs". Across the road is the Memorial Building
of Clare built in grey brick and completed in 1934. This
new Clare building was the first example of a college
expanding to the other side of the "Backs". Immediately to the west of it is the University Library, the
most impressive university building which Cambridge
has seen for some hundreds of years. Individual impres-
sions may vary, but certainly it is planned on a scale
greater than that of any other building in Cambridge.
The central tower, 156 feet high, commands a view of
the town and the surrounding country unknown before.
But the tower is not designed for sightseers; it is designed, like the rest of the building, for holding books.
By contrast with the cramped conditions of the old
library the million and a quarter volumes are arranged
in the decency and order which they deserve, and the site
allows for wide expansion of the building in future years.
Further, the Reading Room and the Anderson Room[1]
make generous provision for the needs of students

[1] Named in memory of the late Sir Hugh Anderson, Master of
Gonville and Caius, to whose activity the initiation of the scheme
for the new Library was mainly due.

and readers. The main entrance to the Library is from West Road, which runs westward from the Backs to Grange Road, and inevitably it is, for most, a longer journey to the new building than to the old; but this inconvenience is outweighed by the immense advantage of having all the books under one roof.

In Grange Road is Selwyn College, which since its foundation in 1882 has grown rapidly both in numbers and in fabric. The chapel was built in 1895, and the range of buildings on the south containing the hall and combination room was finished in 1909. Just beyond Selwyn is Newnham College, which was gradually developed round the Old Hall, built in 1875. Sidgwick Hall, Clough Hall, Kennedy Buildings, and Peile Hall have since been added and further extensions have quite recently been made. The bronze entrance gates are a memorial to the first Principal, Miss A. J. Clough. East of Newnham is Ridley Hall, a theological college, founded in 1879 by members of the Evangelical party in the Church of England. From the cross-roads just below Ridley Hall, Queens' Road leads back to Clare, and alongside the Old Court of Clare stands Trinity Hall. Between two external walls of the college is a small triangular garden-plot. It was planted by Joseph Jowett, Professor of Civil Law, at the end of the eighteenth century, and the "little garden Jowett made" was commemorated in an epigram of which there are many variants. Three sides of the original court (containing hall, kitchen and chapel) remain, though they have been much altered by being faced with stone in the eighteenth century. The library of the college, built in Elizabeth's reign, is one of the most interesting in Cambridge; only minor alterations have been made in it and chained books may still be seen.

Nearly opposite the entrance gateway of Trinity Hall is Senate-House Passage, which runs between the Senate-House and Gonville and Caius College. At the east end of this passage we are near the heart of the town as well as of the university. Opposite is the church of St Mary the Great (originally St Mary-by-the-Market), where University Sermons are preached. The church was largely rebuilt at the end of the fifteenth century and the university bore the greater part of the expense. Since then the church has been much altered. Its chimes are famous and were composed by Dr Jowett, of Trinity Hall, about 1790.[1] Behind Great St Mary's is Market Hill,[2] which in earlier centuries was covered with shops and houses. Now there is an open square where markets are regularly held. Just to the north of Senate-House Passage is the entrance to Gonville and Caius College. When John Caius obtained a royal licence in 1557 to re-found his old college, he not only prepared a new set of statutes, but also planned an extension of the college buildings. The old college consisted of a single court

[1] These "Cambridge chimes" are frequently, but wrongly, referred to as "the Westminster chimes".

[2] "Hill" signifies simply a rise in the ground above the level of the adjoining fen. Cf. Peas Hill.

(still known as Gonville Court), and Caius built his court to the south of it. The south side, however, he would not build "lest the air, from being confined within a narrow space, should become foul". His love of symbolism is seen in his three gates: the Gate of Humility at the entrance to the college, the Gate of Virtue at the entrance of the New Court, and the Gate of Honour on the south side of the court. This last gate was meant to symbolise the student's entry into successful disputation in the Schools. Both the Gate of Virtue and the Gate of Honour remain in their beauty, but the old Gate of Humility stands in the Master's Garden, having been swept away by the Gothic enthusiasm which is responsible for the present appearance of Gonville and Caius College from the street. The college has also spread to the other side of the street in buildings which partially encircle St Michael's Church. This church was rebuilt in the fourteenth century by Hervey de Stanton, founder of Michaelhouse. Having no chapel for his scholars, he was granted the appropriation of the church, and planned it as a collegiate parish church, the large chancel being designed as a collegiate quire. In the middle of this chancel is the founder's tomb.

Michaelhouse originally stood to the north-west of Gonville Hall and gave its name to the narrow lane (St Michael's Lane) which, under the name of Trinity Lane, now divides Caius from Trinity. King's Hall, one of the other foundations absorbed by Henry VIII in 1546, stood on what is now the north-eastern corner of the Great Court of Trinity, and its entrance gateway now forms part of the Great Gate, on which Edward III and his sons, as well as Henry VIII, are commemorated. The chapel was completed in 1564, and under the mastership of Thomas Nevile the Great Court began to assume its present magnificence. Portions of King's Hall were destroyed; the ancient gate of King Edward III was set back to range with the chapel; a new gateway, the Queen's Gate, was built in honour of Elizabeth on the south; the hall, whose proportions were based upon those of the hall of the Middle Temple, was designed by Ralph Symons. Nevile's name is more closely linked with the court which he built at his own expense to the west of the hall, and later, across the end of it, Sir Christopher Wren built the library—"certainly one of the very greatest works of the great master of English architecture". The library contains some famous manuscripts— Milton's *Lycidas*, etc., Thackeray's *Esmond*, Tennyson's *In Memoriam*. In the ante-chapel may be seen statues of some of Trinity's great scholars—Francis Bacon and Isaac Newton among them:

"The antechapel where the statue stood
Of Newton with his prism and silent face,
The marble index of a mind for ever
Voyaging through strange seas of Thought, alone".[1]

St John's College, which stands next to Trinity, is entered through a noble gateway tower, on which the foundress is commemorated by the Beaufort antelopes

[1] Wordsworth, *The Prelude*.

43

and a row of *marguerites*. The first court, which belongs
to the period of the foundation of the college, has unfortunately suffered at the hands of architectural im-
provers. The chapel and the master's lodging on the
north side were pulled down in 1869 and replaced by an
elaborately Gothic chapel designed by Sir Gilbert Scott.
On the south side the brickwork was faced with stone in
the eighteenth century. Another noble gateway leads to
the second court, built in the sixteenth century by means
of a benefaction from the Countess of Shrewsbury. On
the upper floor of the north side of this court is one of
the most famous rooms in Cambridge—the combination
room, originally the gallery of the old master's lodging,
with panelled walls and a richly plastered ceiling.

Beyond this court is yet another, with the library (a
beautiful building erected in 1624) on its north side. The
west side of the court overlooks the river, and the college
has two bridges, the Old Bridge, built by Robert Grumbold in 1696, and the "Bridge of Sighs", an "ingeniously
contrived" bridge of 1831, which leads to the rambling
neo-Gothic pile on the other side of the river. Very recently a new and dignified range of buildings has been
completed between the chapel and Bridge Street. It was
from St John's that Wordsworth looked out upon

"Gowns grave, or gaudy, doctors, students, streets,
 Courts, cloisters, flocks of churches, gateways, towers".

At the end of the old High Street (which is now successively Trumpington Street, King's Parade, Trinity

Street, St John's Street) there stands one of the most interesting of the "flocks of churches". It is the church of the Holy Sepulchre, one of the four round churches in England[1] and belonging probably to the early twelfth century. Behind it are the premises of the Union Society, a debating society of respectable antiquity, open to the whole university and possessing a fine library and other amenities.

Bridge Street leads from the Round Church to the bridge which was originally a vital means of communication between East Anglia and the Midlands. Just beyond it is Magdalene College. In the first court are the chapel and the hall; though they have been much altered, these belong to the original Buckingham College. In the second court the Pepysian Library commemorates the most famous of Magdalene men. Samuel Pepys, who entered the college in 1651, was an enthusiastic collector of books and prints and provided in his will that his books should go to his own college and that they should be kept in what was then "the new building". The library also contains the six quarto volumes of the *Diary*. Recently new Magdalene buildings have arisen on the other side of the road, where a small court is named after George Mallory, fellow of the college, who lost his life on Mount Everest.

Beyond Magdalene is the only hill in Cambridge—Castle Hill, near the top of which is a defensive mound possibly belonging to the British period and certainly

[1] The other three are the Temple Church in London, St Sepulchre's in Northampton, and Little Maplestead Church in Essex.

occupied by the Romans. The castle built by William I was, in part, a ruin as early as the fifteenth century, and now but few traces of it remain. Past the castle the road leads in a straight Roman line to Huntingdon, and about two miles along it is Girton College. Since the first portion of the building rose in 1873 the college has greatly expanded, and the buildings now include hall, library, chapel, lecture-rooms and other appurtenances of college life.

East of the Round Church is a turning off Bridge Street called Jesus Lane, leading to Jesus College, which, alone amongst Cambridge colleges, preserves the monastic plan of the religious foundation which it replaced. The nunnery church, with its fine Norman and Early English windows, was reduced in size, but remains the college chapel; the cloisters are preserved, and the hall, with cellars beneath, is on the site of the old refectory. The entrance gateway, built at the end of a walled approach known as "the Chimney", is a noble piece of brickwork, and a statue of Bishop Alcock stands in the centre of it. Jesus College is fortunate in having a grove large enough to contain its playing-fields. Beyond these fields is Midsummer Common (where Midsummer Fair is held), and beyond the Common is the Cam, with the college boat-houses lining the opposite bank.

Immediately to the south of Jesus College is Wesley House, a training college for the Wesleyan ministry built in 1927; and opposite is Westcott House, a clergy training school founded in 1881 in memory of Bishop Westcott.

46

South of Westcott House is Sidney Sussex College, built in 1598, on the site of a Franciscan friary. The original building was of brick, but was much altered and enlarged in the eighteenth and nineteenth centuries. Sidney has one of the most interesting chapels in Cambridge. Shortly after the foundation of the college, the old Franciscan refectory was adapted for use as a chapel. In 1780 this was replaced by a new building, and in 1912 the eighteenth-century chapel was enlarged and transformed with plaster ceiling, panels of richly carved oak and marble floor. Oliver Cromwell entered the college in 1616, and in the hall is the portrait traditionally associated with the Protector's request that the painter should "remark all these roughnesses, pimples, warts, and everything as you see me".

Beyond the end of Sidney Street is Christ's College, founded as God's House by Henry VI and "augmented finished and stablished" by the Lady Margaret.[1] Its gateway is naturally similar to that of St John's, but the whole front of the college was refaced in the eighteenth century, owing to the dilapidated state of the original clunch and brickwork. The first court, though also refaced, remains as it was planned, and contains hall, chapel, master's lodge (of which part was originally reserved for the foundress), buttery and scholars' chambers. In the second court are the Fellows' Buildings, "a very noble erection" belonging to the middle of the seventeenth century. In the famous garden of Christ's there

[1] See Dr A. H. Lloyd's *Early History of Christ's College*.

is a mulberry tree associated with the most famous of Christ's men—John Milton, who entered the college in 1625. It is probable that the tree has no more direct connection with the poet than has the Pembroke mulberry with Spenser; but the legend persists. Certainly the trees were planted early in the seventeenth century. There have been many famous Christ's men since Milton, and in the early nineteenth century the greatest of them was Charles Darwin.

Christ's College stands opposite the church of St Andrew the Great, and the street in which it stands is St Andrew's Street. Further along the same street is Emmanuel College. The college was built on the site of a Dominican house, and the Dominican church became the hall of the college. A chapel (afterwards converted into a library) was built to run north and south, perhaps as a Puritan protest. But later, in 1665, William Sancroft, Master of the College, employed Sir Christopher Wren to build a new chapel in the middle of the east side of the court. It is joined to the court by cloisters, and above the cloisters is a gallery leading to the master's lodge. Emmanuel also has a north court on the other side of the narrow lane known as Emmanuel Street, and the old and the new courts are linked by a subway. Emmanuel was the home of most of the Cambridge Platonists in the seventeenth century, and Richard Farmer (Master in 1775) was finely representative of what was best in Cambridge scholarship and social life in the eighteenth century.

On the other side of the road, which has now become

Regent Street, is Downing College, of which the first buildings were begun in 1807. The architect was William Wilkins, who planned "one large stone-faced quadrangle, more spacious than that of Trinity College". But only the east and west sides were built, and so the college remained for over a hundred years. Recently, however, two new blocks (built, like the other parts, of Ketton stone) have been completed on the north side, and between them there is left room for the buildings of a library and a chapel in the future. The original site of Downing was magnificent in extent. Unfortunately financial difficulties at the end of the nineteenth century compelled the college to sell the northern portion of its land to the university. The university has made full use of it. The "Downing Site", that is the land between the college and Downing Street, has become a symbol of the expansion of scientific learning and research in Cambridge. Facing Downing Street are the Sedgwick Museum of Geology, the Law School, and the Museum of Archaeology and Ethnology. Round the corner, in Tennis Court Road, are the Biochemistry and Pathology buildings; in the middle of the site are the schools of Botany, Agriculture, Physiology, and Psychology; nearer to the college boundary are those of Parasitology and Geography, with a Low Temperature Station between them. All these buildings have been erected in the present century. On the north side of Downing Street is a group of buildings which have grown on a site which has older associations with natural science. It was the site, in the Middle Ages, of an Augustinian

R   49   4 friary; in 1760 it was bought by Dr Walker, Vice-Master of Trinity, and given to the university for a Botanic Garden. In 1852 this garden was transferred to a site on the Trumpington Road[1] and gradually the "Botanic Garden site" was allotted to the heads of various scientific faculties. To-day Chemistry and Medicine have buildings on the street front; behind them are the laboratories and museums of Zoology, Mineralogy, and Anatomy. The Engineering School had its laboratory here until 1921, when the laboratory was removed to a new building on the edge of Coe Fen and the old building was adapted to the needs of Physical Chemistry.

The entrance to the Cavendish Laboratory of Experimental Physics is on the east side of Free School Lane, the older part of the building having been erected in 1874. Behind it is a new Arts School, containing lecture-rooms, the library of the Philosophical Society and a large Examination School built in 1909 with special care for lighting and ventilation "which are so important to the mental equilibrium of the examination candidates".

Downing College is bounded on the west by Tennis Court Road, out of which Fitzwilliam Street leads straight to Fitzwilliam House, the headquarters of the non-collegiate body, and the Fitzwilliam Museum. The museum grew out of a bequest of money as well as of pictures, prints, manuscripts, and books made to the university by Viscount Fitzwilliam in 1816. The original building was designed in the classical style by George

[1] The iron gates at the entrance to the present garden were moved from the old site.

Basevi and was begun in 1837. Basevi, however, did not live to see his work completed, being killed by a fall in Ely Cathedral, and the work was carried on by C. R. Cockerell. The collections were installed in 1848, but the main building was not completed until 1875. In recent years large additions to the building have been made—the Marlay Galleries, built in 1924 to hold the munificent bequest of Charles Brinsley Marlay, the Courtauld Extension (1931) due to a benefaction of the Courtauld family, and a further extension (1936) of three galleries, including the Charrington Print Room.

The Fitzwilliam Museum covers a wide field of interest. The English pictures include works by Hogarth, Reynolds, Gainsborough, Romney, Blake, and Turner, as well as work by the Pre-Raphaelites and contemporary painters; there are two Titians and a Paolo Veronese as well as examples of earlier Italian painting; there is Rembrandt's *Man in a Plumed Hat* and the *Village Festival* of the younger Peter Brueghel. Amongst the medieval manuscripts is the Metz Pontifical and the music includes the Fitzwilliam Virginal Book; the Glaisher room is devoted to the great collection of English and continental pottery bequeathed by J. W. L. Glaisher in 1928. In addition there are classical and Egyptian galleries, a coin room, a library, and a large collection of autograph music.

On its north side the Fitzwilliam adjoins the lovely deer park of Peterhouse, now, alas, without its deer.

So, in a rough and ready way, the perambulation is complete.

III

ACADEMICA

In the barest outline we have surveyed seven centuries of university history and have cast a rapid glance at the university and college buildings which those centuries have produced. How is the university organised and governed to-day? Though the university is older than the oldest college, it is now "almost impossible to conceive of the university apart from the colleges". Through the colleges, which are themselves corporate bodies managing their own affairs, the university is supplied with its personnel; and while there are a few members of the university who do not belong to a college, every member of a college is a member of the university, and the normal candidate for entrance to the university must be admitted either through a college or as an approved non-collegiate student. The regulations for this formal admission, or matriculation, are a good example of the interaction of university and college. In the first place, the university accepts for matriculation only those who have already been admitted to a college or to the non-collegiate body; in the second place, the university requires that before a candidate may come into residence in a college he shall have passed the "Previous", that is, the university entrance examination; in the third place, even when he has satisfied the university examiners, the college may also require him to pass a college entrance examination.

In this way some 1700 undergraduates (that is, students who have not "graduated", or taken a degree) enter the university through the colleges every year. At the end of three years the majority of these will proceed to the degree of Bachelor of Arts and so become "graduate" members of the university; in the fourth year thereafter many of these will proceed, without any further examination, to the degree of Master of Arts,[1] and of these there will be some who have obtained teaching or administrative posts in the university or in a college or in both.

Thus the whole body of graduates is divided into two classes: (1) a very large class of non-resident members of the university; (2) a much smaller class of resident teachers and administrators. Those in the first class become members of the Senate of the University, those in the second class are qualified to become members of the Regent House. It is to this latter body that the govern-

---

[1] Since the organisation of Triposes, the *quadrivium* has become simply a period of time. The higher degrees (that is, Doctorates of Divinity, Law, Medicine, Science, Letters, Music, Philosophy as well as the Bachelorship of Divinity and the Masterships of Music, Science and Letters) are obtained by the writing of theses. (See pp. 92, 97.) The Mastership of Surgery is obtained by examination.

ment of the university now in practice belongs.[1] It should, however, be made clear that the statutes of the university rest upon the authority, not of the Regent House or of the Senate, but of the King in Council and of Parliament. All legislative proposals put before the university must fulfil one condition—they must not infringe the Statutes. Subject to this condition, the university makes its own laws, or Ordinances.

The Senate of the University still has certain powers: it elects the Chancellor and some other officers and it votes upon certain kinds of proposals or "Graces"[2] which are brought before the university; but, for the most part, Graces are approved by the Regent House, subject to appeal to the Senate under certain conditions.

A large number of the Graces put before the Regent House are proposals to approve recommendations contained in reports by various university bodies. Among the more important of these are the following:

(1) The Council of the Senate, which took the place of the *caput senatus* in 1856, consists of the Chancellor, the Vice-Chancellor, and sixteen graduates elected by the

[1] The creation, or re-creation, of the Regent House dates from the statutes of 1926. Before that, the non-resident Master of Arts had a share in university legislation equal to that of the resident, and when any controversy of wide interest (e.g. Women's Degrees or Compulsory Greek) was before the Senate large numbers of non-residents came up to Cambridge to vote.

[2] From the Latin *Gratia*, the term used in the Middle Ages and long after. Latin was the official language of the university until the nineteenth century and still survives in certain formulae.

Regent House.[1] By long-standing custom, however, the Chancellor is a distinguished non-resident and is present only on ceremonial occasions.[2] Consequently the active head of the university is the Vice-Chancellor, who is elected annually from among the Heads of Colleges and is *ex officio* chairman of a large number of university bodies.[3] The Council of the Senate is the channel through which all Graces to be submitted to the university must first pass; it also nominates members to be appointed by Grace to serve on other university bodies. The Council has a permanent secretary in the person of the Registrary, whose duty it is to keep records of the proceedings of the university, to preserve such records in the Registry, to attend all meetings (or "Congregations") of the Senate and of the Regent House, and to edit the official gazette of the university.

(2) The Financial Board, which is responsible for the management of the property, the income, and the expenditure of the university, consists of the Vice-Chancellor and ten members of the Senate, four being members

[1] Four of the sixteen must be Heads of Colleges and four Professors or Readers.

[2] The Chancellor of the Middle Ages held office only for a year or two. Since the election of Bishop Fisher in 1504 the practice has been to elect a Chancellor for life. Recent Chancellors have been: The Duke of Devonshire (1892), Lord Rayleigh (1908), Lord Balfour (1919), Lord Baldwin (1930).

[3] It would be impossible for the Vice-Chancellor to preside over all these bodies, and he normally delegates the chairmanship of most except the Council of the Senate, the Financial Board, and the General Board.

of the Council, four elected by representatives of the
colleges, and two nominated by the Council and appointed by the Regent House. The board receives, for
approval, the financial estimates of the various university
departments, publishes annual accounts relating both to
the university as a whole and to the individual colleges;
it collects the contributions due from the colleges towards the expenses of the university; it makes recommendations to the university for the purchase or the sale
of real property; it administers a large number of trust
funds created as the result of benefactions and bequests;
it is in fact the central financial body of the university.
The Treasurer of the University, a permanent official,
acts as its secretary.

(3) The General Board of the Faculties, whose duty,
in general, is to advise the university as to educational
policy, consists of the Vice-Chancellor and twelve members, of whom not less than four must be members of the
Council. The board supervises the work of the various
teaching faculties, approves the schedules of teaching
and lecturing submitted by the faculties, and appoints
examiners. It has a permanent secretary with the title
Secretary General of the Faculties.

It is in the hands of these three bodies that the pre-
paratory work of university legislation chiefly lies; but
there are, in addition, a large number of other delibera-
tive bodies. Each of the faculties has its board, and of the
faculties there are twenty, divided into four groups. In
the first group are Classics, Divinity, English, Fine Arts,

Modern and Medieval Languages, Music, Oriental Languages; in the second, Economics and Politics, History, Law, Moral Science; in the third, Engineering, Geography and Geology, Mathematics, Physics and Chemistry; in the fourth, Agriculture, Archaeology and Anthropology, Biology 'A', Biology 'B', Medicine. Each of the Faculty Boards makes recommendations to the General Board with respect to teaching, lecturing and examining and has the right to present reports to the university. There are also many other boards and syndicates which are entrusted with the control of various departments and institutions; such as the Board of Research Studies, which supervises the work of students who after taking a degree proceed to engage in research; the Board of Extra-Mural Studies, which directs the courses of study arranged for students outside the university; the Local Examinations Syndicate, which controls the "Cambridge Local" school examinations held at various centres throughout the Empire; the Syndicates which control such institutions as the University Library, the University Press, the Fitzwilliam Museum, the Botanic Garden. These boards and syndicates manage their respective departments in accordance with the powers assigned to them by the University Ordinances; in some cases they appoint their own secretaries and permanent officials. Like the other boards, they have the right to make reports to the university, and it is in such reports that university legislation is for the most part initiated. After approval by the Council of the Senate,

57

the reports are published in the official journal of the university, the *Cambridge University Reporter*; opportunity is then given to the Senate to discuss them; no vote is taken at these discussions, but the expression of serious criticism often results in the report being referred back to the body concerned and in the issue of an amended report; subsequently the Regent House is offered a Grace embodying the recommendations. An examination of a typical series of Graces submitted to a Congregation of the Regent House and all taken from a single number of the *Cambridge University Reporter*, may serve as a convenient illustration:

That the recommendations contained in the Report of the Council of the Senate dated..., on certain regulations concerning women students be approved.

That the recommendations contained in the Report of the General Board, dated..., on the position of the subject Anatomy in the University be approved.

That the recommendation contained in the Report of the Buildings Syndicate, dated..., on a site for the extension of the Museum of Archaeology and of Ethnology be approved.

That the recommendation contained in the Report of the Library Syndicate, dated..., on additional staff needed in the new Library be approved.

That the recommendations contained in the Report of the Faculty Board of Mathematics, dated..., on a proposed alteration in the regulations for the Mathematical Tripos Part III be approved.

That Professor...be appointed to represent the University on...at the Hundredth Anniversary of the Foundation of the Medical School of the University of Liverpool.

That...of...College, be allowed to complete the requirements for the Ordinary B.A. Degree by passing either Part of the General Examination.

That, on the nomination of the General Board, with the concurrence of the Council of the Senate,...of...College be appointed Secretary General of the Faculties.

The formal presentation of such Graces is made at a Congregation in the Senate-House, the Vice-Chancellor presiding. Degrees are also conferred at a Congregation, and the visitor who has entered the Senate-House in order to see the ceremony of the conferment of degrees may well be puzzled at hearing what seems to him a rapid recitation of a number of formal propositions by an official who raises his hat and says "Placet" at intervals. Actually, the visitor is witnessing the final stage of university legislation. The official who reads each Grace aloud is one of the Proctors, and, unless he hears anything to the contrary, the Proctor will himself declare "Placet" (i.e. Approved) after the recital. But any member of the Regent House, by saying "Non placet", may call for a vote. The supporters, or Placets, move to one side of the house, the opponents, or Non-placets, to the other. If the majority for either side is an obvious one, the Proctor declares "Placet" or "Non placet"; but, if demanded by not less than ten members, a scrutiny is taken and when the question is one that has aroused keen controversy, each member present is provided with a "Placet" or "Non-placet" card on which he writes his name. Hitherto the voting has always been open; but provision exists for a ballot in the Senate-House.

In the Senate-House the continuity of university office and university ceremonial is well exemplified. The office of Proctor, as has already been noted, dates back to the early fourteenth century, and in spite of the curtailment of their powers under the Elizabethan statutes they remain the principal disciplinary officers of the university, patrolling the streets at night in the interests of good order and having the right to enter licensed premises and places of public entertainment. They also retain their ancient insignia, the Senior Proctor's being a linstock and small partizan, the Junior Proctor's a halberd and a butter measure.[1] These weapons are carried on ceremonial occasions by the Proctor's "men" or "constables", commonly selected from among the more stalwart college servants. These "bull-dogs", as they are popularly called, assist in the prevention and detection of undergraduate misdemeanours and are provided by the University with a suitable livery. The Proctors attend the university sermon in full state, carrying ancient volumes

[1] Butter was, until recently, sold in Cambridge by the yard. See the illustration facing p. 83.

60

THE ORATOR

of statutes; it is their duty to read Graces at Congregations of the Senate and of the Regent House, and at the beginning of each academical year (the first of October) they admit the incoming Vice-Chancellor to office.[1]

The office of Orator was founded in 1522. The Orator's duty is to write addresses and formal letters on behalf of the university and to present to the Chancellor, or Vice-Chancellor, the recipients of honorary degrees. It is in this last capacity that the Orator is chiefly known to the public. While the ordinary recipient of a degree is presented by a representative of his college or his faculty, the recipient of an honorary degree is presented by the Orator, who recites a Latin speech in his honour.

Another ancient office is that of Esquire Bedell. Their number was originally three, but this was reduced to two by the statutes of 1858. Like other officials, they are graduate members of the university, and their duty is to attend the Chancellor or Vice-Chancellor on public occasions in the Senate-House and elsewhere. In processions the Bedells walk in front of the Chancellor or Vice-Chancellor carrying the silver maces presented to the university by the Duke of Buckingham, Chancellor, in 1626. The mace of the Yeoman Bedell (an office abolished in 1858) is now carried by the University Marshal.

Such are a few features of the administrative, legislative and ceremonial machinery of modern Cambridge. Such machinery is a means, not an end—a means to the

[1] The offices of Proctor and Esquire Bedell are the only ones from which women are to be excluded.

promotion of sound learning. The elaboration of the machinery is due in part to the growth in the numbers of students, in part to the widening of the bounds of learning. The mere list of the twenty faculties, several of which are divided into departments,[1] presents a marked contrast with the curriculum either of the Middle Ages or of the early nineteenth century. For the conduct of its teaching the university appoints seventy-six professors[2] and twenty-seven readers, who co-operate with the professors in the various subjects; and each Faculty has its staff of lecturers or demonstrators. With a few exceptions the professors are appointed by electoral boards, the chairman being the Vice-Chancellor and the members being appointed by the university.[3] Readers, lecturers, and demonstrators are appointed by a committee of the faculty concerned. Of the resident graduates who thus direct the course of university business and university teaching a large number are also concerned in the government of a particular college.

Like the university, each college has its statutes resting on the authority of the King in Council and of Parliament. These statutes provide in detail for the form of

[1] Thus Biology 'A' includes Botany, Entomology, Mycology, Parasitology, Zoology; Biology 'B' includes Anatomy, Biochemistry, Experimental Psychology, Pathology, Physiology.

[2] 41 professorships have been founded in the present century.

[3] On each of these boards there must be two members who have no official connection with the university.

government of the college, for the election of master, fellows, scholars and servants, for the administration of college property, for the audit of college accounts, for the regulation of chapel services, and for various other matters. As with the university, such regulations as are made by the college from time to time must not contravene the statutes. If the college wishes to amend an existing statute or introduce a new one, the Council of the Senate considers whether the statute affects the university, and, if it does, proposes a Grace for giving or withholding the university's consent; if not, or if the university's consent is given, the college must then submit the new statute for approval by His Majesty in Council. The governing body of a college is normally "the Master and Fellows". The word "Fellow", a translation of the Latin *socius*, dates back to the earliest set of Cambridge college statutes, which provided for "a Master and fourteen perpetual Fellows, studiously engaged in the pursuit of literature". These "Fellows" were students, who were supported on the foundation, as opposed to "pensioners", who were at a later date admitted to colleges on condition of their paying for their board, lodging, and instruction. The early statutes of Pembroke provided for the support of thirty scholars, more or less, of whom twenty-four, denominated fellows, were to be greater and permanent. In modern times the distinction between a "fellow" and a "scholar" has in all colleges become much wider. A scholar is normally a member of the college who, before coming into residence,

63

has been elected to a scholarship on the result of an open competitive examination conducted by the college. As a scholar he becomes entitled to a set of rooms in college and to certain emoluments which are in fact applied to the reduction of fees; subject to good work and conduct, he remains a scholar throughout his time as an undergraduate and sometimes as a Bachelor of Arts. A fellow, on the other hand, is normally a man who has taken the degree of Bachelor of Arts or some higher degree and has been elected to a fellowship with a view to teaching, or administration or research. As a fellow, he receives his "dividend", or share of the college revenues, and additional emoluments for any college office to which he may be appointed; he is also allotted rooms in college and is provided with dinner at the fellows' (or "high") table in the college hall. As a fellow, he has, in nearly all cases, a share in the government of the college. As has been noted earlier, no fellow is now elected for life. Normally he is elected for three years; his re-election very often depending on whether he has been appointed to a college or university office in the meantime.

In any one college it will usually be found that a certain number of the fellows have been undergraduate members of the college. The proportion varies according to circumstance and college tradition, but a college is normally free, and exercises its freedom, to elect a graduate member of another college, sometimes of a college in the University of Oxford.

In nearly all colleges the master is elected by the

fellows.[1] Here, again, while it frequently happens that the fellows elect one of themselves, it is by no means unusual for a master to be chosen from another college. The master of a college receives a stipend and is also provided with "lodgings" or a lodge, that is, a house within the college precincts in which he may live with his family.

The master, fellows and scholars thus constitute the heart of the personnel of a college, being supported, in whole or in part, on the college foundation. Numerically, however, by far the largest class in any college is that of the undergraduates who are not scholars. Such undergraduates do not, of course, receive any emolument from the college;[2] in other words, they pay their bills in full. But apart from this and from certain minor privileges, the social status of the ordinary undergraduate is, for all practical purposes, the same as that of the scholar.[3]

The colleges vary very widely in size and wealth; the foundation may provide for sixty fellows or for ten.

[1] The exceptions are Trinity, of which the mastership is a Crown appointment; Magdalene, of which the mastership is in the gift of the Barony of Braybrooke as representing the founder; and Selwyn, whose master is elected by a council containing a number of members outside the college.

[2] There is, however, a class of "exhibitioners", who are awarded small emoluments on the result of the scholarship examination, but are not technically on the foundation.

[3] The scholar of a college has no distinctive gown, as he has in Oxford; in Cambridge the undergraduate gowns are distinguished as by colleges; e.g. the Caius undergraduate wears a blue gown with a velvet collar; a Clare gown is black, with velvet chevrons. The gowns worn by B.A.'s and holders of higher degrees are of a uniform pattern prescribed by the university.

Accordingly the colleges with large foundations delegate
the administration to a council, elected from among the
fellows.

Each college, as has been said, is a separate corporation and jealously guards its autonomy. But here the
closeness of the relation between the university and the
colleges is again exemplified. Each college is obliged
by university statute to make an annual contribution to
university funds, the amount being calculated as a percentage of the college income and the percentage being
increased upon the incomes of the richer colleges. The
colleges are also required to present their annual accounts
to the university in a prescribed form.

Further, while each college is entirely free to elect its
own scholars provided that it does so by means of an open
competitive examination held for the purpose, and is also
free to elect its fellows with or without an examination,
the university requires first, that among its fellows a
college shall maintain a quota (varying from two to nine
according to the size and wealth of the foundation) of
university professors; and, secondly, that there shall be
among the fellows a certain nicely calculated proportion
who are holders of a readership, lectureship, demon-
stratorship or certain other offices in the university.

Thus it is now virtually impossible for the fellows of a
college as a whole to be detached from the university. On
the other hand, the college is entirely free in the appointment of its officers for the administration of its own affairs
and for the teaching of its own undergraduates within the

66

college precincts. These officers are normally the Vice-Master or President, the Tutor, the Dean, the Bursar, the Steward, the Praelector, the Librarian, and the Lecturers.

The Vice-Master, or President, acts as the Master's deputy in his absence and in a few colleges performs some other duties.

The Tutor is the pivot of the college system as that system is worked in Cambridge. He has normally a considerable voice in the acceptance or rejection of candidates for admission to the college; when the candidate has become his pupil, he stands *in loco parentis* to him and advises him not only about his studies, " but also on every kind of problem arising out of college and university life on which a young man is likely to need counsel ". The increase in numbers in recent years has made it necessary for nearly every college to have more than one tutor, the number varying according to the size of the college.

The Dean is normally a fellow of the college in Holy Orders who is responsible for the conduct of services in the college chapel. Until recently attendance at a prescribed number of services was compulsory in all colleges, but compulsion has now been abandoned. Matins and evensong, however, are still said or sung daily in college chapels in term time. In some colleges there is also a "Dean of College", who is responsible for the preservation of discipline within the precincts of the college.

The Bursar is responsible for the control of college property, college servants and college finance and prepares the accounts for annual audit; the Steward supervises the college hall and kitchen and the considerable accounting which they involve.[1]

The Praelector (or Father of the College) has the duty of presenting members of the college for degrees, and the Librarian is entrusted with the custody of the manuscripts and printed books belonging to the college.

Of these offices the majority are generally held by fellows of the college, but the post of steward or librarian may well be held by one who is not a fellow.

While these college offices—and especially the tutorship and bursarship—are of vital importance in the college economy, none of them are necessarily "wholetime" offices in the sense of precluding their holders from engaging in the work of teaching. On the contrary, a large proportion of the holders of college offices are also college lecturers in their own subjects. If a college cannot provide a lecturer in any particular subject from among its fellows, it appoints either a graduate member of the college who is not a fellow or a member of another college to act as lecturer and supervisor in that subject. Thus the teaching staff of a college is commonly a larger body than that of the fellows, and while the additional lecturers and supervisors take no part in the government of the college, they are frequently invited to share its social amenities; a college lecturer is naturally provided with a room in which he can teach and is usually given the privilege of dining with the fellows at the "high table" in hall.

[1] The allotment of responsibility to the financial officers varies in different colleges.

68

The care with which college teaching is organised rests upon the tradition that, while the university may properly control the provision of lectures, it is upon the colleges that the responsibility rests for personal supervision.[1]

The working of this dual system of instruction is facilitated by the fact that there is no sharp division between the personnel of university lecturers on the one hand and that of college teachers on the other. One man, of course, may spend a great deal more time in giving university lectures than in personal instruction in his own rooms in college, and *vice versa*. But, in teaching as in administration, the combination of university and college functions in the person of a single fellow of a college is the rule rather than the exception. For instance, a fellow of a college may for one hour in the morning be delivering a lecture as university lecturer, say, in the Faculty of Classics; an hour later he may, as college lecturer in the same subject, be taking two of his own pupils in Latin prose; an hour later he may, as assistant tutor, be giving an *exeat* (i.e. leave to go down from college) to a pupil who has been summoned home on urgent domestic business; in the early afternoon he may have to attend a meeting, say, of the General Board or of the Local Examinations Syndicate; later in the afternoon he may be due, as a fellow, at a meeting of the governing body of his own college.

[1] There is, however, a tendency for the university to limit the number of hours which a university lecturer may devote to teaching or administrative work within his own college.

This is not, of course, to suggest that the working day of every fellow of a college or of every university lecturer oscillates so rapidly between college and university. One fellow of a college, not yet burdened with office, may be engaged upon a piece of literary research and may spend the greater part of the day in the University Library; another, recently appointed to a readership in a scientific subject, may be continuously supervising experiments in a laboratory; another, holding one of the financial offices in his college, may after an hour's teaching, devote the rest of the day to college accounts.

The daily occupations of a master of a college may be similarly varied: he may retain some teaching duties in his college or in the university; he may be a member of several university boards and syndicates and may act as the Vice-Chancellor's deputy in the chair of one of them; he may serve on the councils of learned societies; he presides over college meetings and frequently shares with the tutor the work of examining the applications for admission to the college. The days are past when the chief duty of the master of a college could be described as consisting in "consulting his own comfort in a dignified manner".

These few examples do not exhaust the variety of occupation which now characterises the life of the Cambridge don; but they may perhaps serve to show that his life is not necessarily or consistently of the kind that is popularly associated with "the soft obscurities of retirement" and "the shelter of academick bowers".

IV

UNDERGRADUATE

Of the greater part of what has been briefly described in the preceding chapter the undergraduate is happily ignorant. The senior members of the university are to him just "dons", and while from the first he recognises some as responsible for his instruction and discipline, and later reckons some of them among his personal friends, he is not called upon to examine the machinery of government either in his college or in the university.

To become a member of the university, he must first choose his college. A variety of considerations may govern his choice. He may, in the first instance, choose a college because his family or his school or his friends have associations with it. If he has no *a priori* preference of this kind, he will enquire as to the characteristics of individual colleges: he may be attracted by the reputation of a particular tutor or teacher in one college or by the athletic distinction of another. Again, he may base his choice on a preference for a large college to a small college, or *vice versa*. In modern Cambridge, however, the small college containing 50 or 60 undergraduates has ceased to exist. The smallest colleges (Peterhouse, Corpus Christi and Selwyn) have about 160 undergraduates each; five colleges (King's, Trinity Hall, Magdalene, Sidney Sussex, Downing) have between 180 and 260 each; another eight (Clare, Pembroke, Queens', Christ's, Jesus, Emmanuel, Gonville and Caius, St Catharine's) have between 280 and 330 each; St John's has 430, and Trinity 670; there are also about 200 non-collegiate undergraduates, the majority of whom are members of Fitzwilliam House.

A candidate for a college whose scholastic ability justifies him in sitting for an entrance scholarship makes his choice of a college in entering himself as a scholarship candidate. Three groups of colleges combine in holding scholarship examinations in December in each year, and a few hold separate examinations in March. A candidate for a scholarship at one of the colleges included in one of the groups states his order of preference in the event of his reaching scholarship standard, and his choice is often governed, in part, by the number of emoluments which any one college is able to offer. If the first college of his choice offers him nothing, he is very often glad to accept a scholarship offered to him by another college. The subjects in which scholarships are normally offered are Mathematics, Classics, Natural Sciences, History, Modern Languages, and English.

The ordinary candidate for entrance, having chosen his college, must ascertain whether the college will accept him. The college will require to be satisfied as to his character and his ability to pass the Previous Examination, supplemented in some cases by a college

72

entrance examination. The Previous Examination (popularly known as the "Little-Go") is in three parts and consists of:

(1) Papers in the following languages, of which two must be taken: Latin, Greek, French, German, Italian, Spanish.

(2) Papers in Mathematics, and Physics and Chemistry.

(3) Papers in English and either in a book of the New Testament or in English History.

The Previous Examination is held four times a year and the different parts may be taken at different times. A large number of entrants, however, obtain exemption from it, either in whole or in part, by examinations passed at school or elsewhere.

With the "Little-Go" or its equivalent safely behind him, the "freshman" will arrive at his college some time during the first week of October. The academical year is divided into three terms—the Michaelmas Term (1 October to 19 December), the Lent Term (5 January to 25 March) and the Easter Term (16 April to 24 June). The freshman has before him a vista of nine terms' residence before he can proceed to a degree; but he is not required to "keep" more than three-quarters of each term and his residence is normally concentrated into a definite period known as Full Term—from October 7–10 to December 5–8, from January 12–16 to March 12–16, and from April 18–23 to June 9–14. Thus the undergraduate's year of residence normally amounts to a little less than six months in all.

73

Before his arrival in Cambridge, the freshman will know where he is to live. While there is no college large enough in extent to house all its undergraduates within its walls, every scholar of a college is allotted rooms in college from the beginning of his residence. Rooms vary considerably in size, but a "set" almost invariably consists of a sitting-room (or "keeping-room") and a bedroom, the latter being sometimes very small.[1] The sets of rooms are mostly grouped on staircases which are entered from the court, and at the entrance to each set there are normally two doors. When the outer door, traditionally built of oak, is shut, it may be assumed either that the occupant is out or that he does not wish to be disturbed— shutting the outer door is known as "sporting the oak".

Some Cambridge colleges, agreeing with the custom which prevails at Oxford, admit their freshmen into college rooms for the first year and send them into lodgings at the end of it; other colleges reverse the order and the undergraduate who is not a scholar of his college will normally live in lodgings for at least part of his time. All lodgings occupied by undergraduates must be "licensed", that is, approved by the Lodging Houses Syndicate. Each college endeavours to secure lodgings for its members quite near the college, but the growth of numbers in recent years has made this difficult. Out of college, as in college, a set of rooms consists of a

[1] In view of the great pressure upon college accommodation in 1946, many undergraduates have now to be content either with a bed-sitting room or with a share of a set of rooms.

sitting-room and a bedroom, and the occupant is subject
to the same control in regard to late hours as the undergraduate in college. The front door of the licensed
lodging-house, like the front gate of the college, must be
locked at 10 p.m. The undergraduate may be let in at
any time up to midnight, a nominal fine being charged
against his account. The landlord or landlady, like the
college porter, is required to report these late entries
to the college authorities, and a too frequent recurrence
of such reports may lead the tutor to take disciplinary
action. Failure to return to college or to lodgings before
midnight, without special leave, is a more serious offence.

Whether living in a college or in lodgings, the undergraduate dines in the college hall in the evening and
may obtain his "commons" (i.e. bread, butter, and milk)
from the college buttery; in recent years, also, many
colleges have adopted the practice of providing a lunch
in hall, which the undergraduate may attend or not as he
likes. Other meals may also be ordered by an undergraduate in college rooms or in lodgings from the college
buttery, but there is no communal meal save dinner in hall.[1]

In lodgings the undergraduate is not required to find
his own furniture; in college rooms he will probably find
the necessary pieces (table, desk, chairs, bookshelf, etc.)
either left for him to buy at a valuation from the outgoing
tenant or provided by the college at a small rent; but he

---

[1] As a result of food-rationing and shortage of labour in
colleges, three meals a day are now (1946) served in hall and
meals cannot be sent to rooms.

75

is, of course, free to supplement them with furniture of his own.

As to costume, he must provide himself with cap, gown, and surplice. Cap and gown must be worn at dinner in hall, at university and college lectures and examinations and also in the streets after dusk; gowns are also worn at ordinary week-day services in chapel, and surplices are worn for chapel by all members of a college on Sundays and Saints' Days and on the evenings before them.

Soon after his arrival the freshman will be requested to call upon his tutor. Allusion has already been made to the importance of the tutor's position in the college system. Every undergraduate is allotted to a tutor; and the tutor is responsible for his welfare, his work, his health, and his general behaviour. It is to the tutor that the parent of an undergraduate turns for information and advice. The tutor is not necessarily the teacher of all his pupils; he is almost always a teacher in his own subject, but many of his pupils may be reading other subjects. To these he recommends teachers and lecturers, from whom he receives reports in due course. Another college official with whom the freshman is brought into contact in his first term is the Praelector, or "Father" of the college. It is he who conducts the freshmen of his college at the beginning of November to the Senate-House and presents them to the Registrary of the University for matriculation. Each signs his name in full in a book kept for the purpose and thereby promises "to observe the

76

Statutes and Ordinances of the University as far as they concern him, and to pay due respect and obedience to the Chancellor and other officers of the University". Among the ordinances which concern him are those relating to the wearing of academical dress and to orderly behaviour in the streets and in lodgings; the university forbids dealings with money-lenders, the discharge of fire-arms, and the lighting of bonfires; it requires that permission shall be obtained from the Junior Proctor before an undergraduate may take part in a dinner or dance or dramatic entertainment in a public place; it forbids an undergraduate in his first year to keep or use a motor vehicle.

The freshman, before coming into residence, will normally have decided upon his course of study. First, he is either a "poll" man or an honours man, that is, he must be a candidate either for the Examinations for the Ordinary Degree or for a Tripos. For the Ordinary Degree he is required to take a "general" examination, the subjects, among which a certain choice can be made, including history, geography, everyday science, and modern languages; and a "special" examination in a selected subject.[1] For an Honours Degree he has a choice of fifteen Triposes.[2] Each of these is a

[1] One of the subjects that may be selected is "Military Studies". A Board of Military Studies supervises the instruction of undergraduates who wish to be candidates for commissions in the Army and the Royal Air Force.

[2] The full list, in order of foundation, is now as follows: Mathematics, Classics, Moral Sciences, Natural Sciences, Theology, Law, History, Oriental Languages, Modern and

77

specialised examination in the subject concerned, but an Honours Degree may be obtained by combining different parts of different Triposes: for example, a student may take the examination for Part I of the Classical Tripos at the end of his first or second year and the examination for Part II of the Historical Tripos at the end of his third year. Owing to the division of all but one of the Triposes into two or more parts, many such combinations are now possible, but it should be made clear that, while the choice of a Tripos will obviously bear some relation to the choice of a career, the course of study for an honours examination in Cambridge is not primarily vocational. Success in a Tripos is not in itself a qualification for entry into one of the learned professions, though it is a valuable help to that end[1].

For the study of Medicine, Music, Agriculture, and Architecture special regulations are made. The examinations for the degree of Bachelor of Medicine are so arranged that the student can pass all but the Final Examination by the end of his third year and then proceed to a hospital in London or elsewhere, returning to Cambridge after another three years to take the Final Examination and to present a thesis for the approval of the Regius Professor of Physic. In addition to this

Medieval Languages, Mechanical Sciences, Economics, Archaeology and Anthropology, English, Geography, Music.

[1] Thus the Council of Legal Education and the Law Society grant certain exemptions to those who have taken honours in the Law Tripos and are proceeding to become barristers or solicitors.

M.B. course, it is usual for medical students to take a part of the Natural Sciences Tripos or the Ordinary Degree examinations in order to obtain, like other students, the degree of B.A. at the end of the third year.[1]

The university course in Agriculture consists of three examinations in agriculture and estate management, and a student who passes all three is entitled to proceed to the Ordinary B.A. Degree. Similarly, a student may obtain the same degree by passing the three examinations in Architectural Studies and the degree of Bachelor of Music may be obtained by passing the two parts of the required examination; it is also possible to combine parts of the musical, the agricultural, or the architectural course with other examinations. Indeed, the variety of combinations of subjects now offered to the student as a means of obtaining a degree adds not a little to the burden of a tutor's work and responsibility. In general, it may be said that the undergraduate with any pretension to scholarly interests will be a candidate for a Tripos. For some years before the war of 1939–45, the number of "poll" men had declined and under present conditions it would be virtually impossible for a candidate for an ordinary degree to gain admission to a college.

Whether "poll" man or honours man, the undergraduate will receive his instruction partly from the university and partly from the college. In the course of

[1] Under the latest regulations (1934) for Medical degrees, the student is obliged to take a Tripos or part of a Tripos.

a day he may attend university lectures for two hours and his college lecturer, or supervisor, for one; or he may spend the greater part of the working day in a laboratory. His teaching, by whatever faculty or department of the university it may be given, is directed by his college and his tutor is responsible for it.

Having planned his lecture-list and having been allotted to a director of his studies, or supervisor, the freshman will find himself in the midst of manifold distractions. Secretaries of athletic clubs in the college will call upon him to enquire whether he intends to row, or to play football or hockey. For membership of any of these clubs he is qualified by the payment of an annual subscription to the Amalgamated Clubs of the college. This payment is not technically compulsory, but in practice every undergraduate welcomes the convenience of joining the college clubs as a whole.[1] Among these he will probably find also a Debating Society open to the whole college, and later he may be elected a member of one of the many private societies within the college at which papers are read and discussed. Membership of a good society of this kind may, without his knowing it, be a valuable part of his education. Outside the college a large number of university organisations are open to him. The largest, the Union Society, offers him a full-dress debate every week together with a good library and the amenities of a club; there is the Officers' Training

[1] At Trinity there is a Field Club which covers all except the rowing clubs.

80

Corps with the various branches of its establishment; there are a number of dramatic societies, of which the oldest is the Amateur Dramatic Club; there are the University Musical Society and the University Music Club; there is the Hawks Club for those who have attained a measure of athletic proficiency; there are clubs and societies to suit nearly every shade of political, religious, and aesthetic opinion; there are clubs for the pursuit of every kind of athletic activity—boxing and fencing, swimming, ice-hockey, cross-country running, archery; there are old-established clubs and there are clubs which were founded yesterday and will die tomorrow. The number of them is bewildering and yet new ones are continually being founded. The freshman will choose in accordance with his interests and will be chosen in accordance with his personality.

About 5000[1] students it is dangerous to generalise; but normally the morning is devoted to work; the student in a literary subject probably attending one or more lectures or classes and the student in a scientific subject spending part of the morning in one of the laboratories. The early afternoon is largely spent in athletic, or other, recreation. The freshman who elects to row is more regularly occupied in the afternoons than others, especially if he becomes a good oar. After steady practice throughout the Michaelmas Term, he will train for the Lent Races, which are rowed in February. The

[1] There were 4849 undergraduates and 483 B.A.'s in residence in the Michaelmas Term 1938.

Cam is narrow and winding and consequently the races between college boats are "bumping" races. About sixteen eight-oared boats are started simultaneously, with two lengths between boat and boat. The object is the "bumping" of the boat in front. As soon as one boat has touched another, both retire from the race and the next day their positions at the start are reversed. There are four days' racing and the order of the boats at the end of the last day's race is preserved as the starting order for the next year. In the Lent Races a college may be represented by a number of boats varying between two and six and each of the seventy boats engaged has the incentive of "going up" so many places on the river. In the May Races (rowed early in June) a smaller number of boats take part, but the best oars in every college are included in the crews, even the heroes who have rowed against Oxford in the previous vacation. The same system of "bumping" is followed and the leading boat at the end of the fourth day's racing is "Head of the River". Later in the evening the boat clubs who have successful celebrate their triumphs in a festive dinner in college known as a "Bump Supper".

Inter-college competition also provides a basis for contests in football, hockey, and athletics. Each college has its playing fields—many of them some distance away from the college itself—and the university has its football ground, its hockey ground and "Fenner's".[1]

[1] Until 1846 the only cricket ground in Cambridge was Parker's Piece, which was acquired by the town in 1613. "Fenner's" was

A BUMP

Phot. Stearn

A JUNIOR PROCTOR
with his "bull-dogs"

Fenner's is the university cricket ground, surrounded by a cinder-track, which is used for athletics during the winter months; alongside it are the university lawn tennis courts. Games between college teams serve also as trials from which those who are to represent the university against Oxford are selected. Every year Oxford and Cambridge teams contend against each other in more than twenty forms of athletic activity. Those who represent the university in the boat race, in cricket, football (Rugby and Association), hockey, athletic sports, and golf obtain their "blues", that is, the right to wear a blazer and other insignia of light blue; representatives of other sports and games (e.g. racquets, swimming, boxing) are awarded "half-blues"[1] and enjoy the minor glory of white blazers with light blue facings. The major contests between Oxford and Cambridge are fought on neutral ground and have of course acquired a fame which stretches far beyond the bounds of either university. The boat race rowed on the Thames in March or April, the cricket match at Lord's in July, the "rugger" match at Twickenham in December are events of national, and international, interest.

But "blues" and "half-blues" are for the few. For the ordinary undergraduate there is plenty of scope for

a private ground opened by the owner, F. P. Fenner, to the university in 1846. It was bought by the university in 1892.

[1] Some of the university teams (e.g. those for lawn tennis and athletic sports) are made up of "blues" and "half-blues", the latter being "second strings".

exercise and enjoyment in college games, and if he has no taste for organised athletics, he is not compelled to take part in them. Squash racquets, fives, lawn tennis and other games afford him plenty of opportunity for taking his exercise as he likes.

Whatever his tastes and capacities may be, the undergraduate will normally get open air and exercise in the afternoon. Between tea and dinner he may sometimes be due at a lecture or a supervision class; the evening is his own and the best opportunity for private work. He will not, of course, always avail himself of it. Meetings of clubs and societies, theatres, concerts, cinemas, as well as informal parties in the rooms of his friends, will present him with continual distractions and he will not savour the full bouquet of Cambridge life if he does not occasionally succumb to them. Gradually he will choose his recreations and his friends, and it should not be difficult for him to reconcile their claims with those of the Tripos for which he is studying. If he too frequently absents himself from lectures and classes, his tutor will reprimand him; but, in the main, he is himself responsible for devoting the proper amount of time to his own reading.

As to formal discipline, he is required to observe two sets of rules—those of the university and those of the college. Rowdiness or other misdemeanour outside the college walls may bring him into contact with a Proctor. A minor offence, such as that of being out of doors after dark without cap and gown, will result in a small fine;

more serious offences are reported to the college tutor. The Proctors have no jurisdiction within the gates of a college, but the college may take disciplinary action as the result of a Proctor's report. A common form of college punishment is "gating", that is, an undergraduate may be forbidden to be outside the college or his lodgings after 10 p.m. or even earlier; a heavier penalty is that of rustication, that is, of being "sent down" either for a term, or a year, or for good.[1]

At the end of his first year, the undergraduate will normally be faced with an examination; if he is reading for honours he will take either a Preliminary Examination or, in some cases, the first part of his Tripos; if he is reading for an Ordinary Degree he will take part of the General or a Special Examination. When the examination is over he will find himself, about the end of the first week in June, in "May Week", the period traditionally allotted to the entertainment of "sisters and cousins". It is in this period that the "May Races" are held on the river on four successive afternoons. On the towing-path the more active supporters run with the boats and shout raucous encouragement to the crew of their college; on the other bank, a more sedate crowd of friends and relations fills the lawns and meadows. Into the evenings of May Week are crowded concerts, dramatic performances, and college balls. The halls and courts, especially of those

[1] The Court of Discipline, a university body composed of the Vice-Chancellor and six Heads of Colleges, also awards sentences of rustication and expulsion.

colleges with a river front, lend themselves to a peculiar beauty of illumination, and college dances are traditionally prolonged until breakfast-time.

The undergraduate's Long Vacation extends from the middle of June to the first week in October. In general, he is free to spend it as he likes, and he may well seize the opportunity to travel abroad, but his tutor naturally expects him to devote at least some portion of it to solid reading. If he can afford it, he will do well to come up to his college for a few weeks between the second week in July and the third week in August. That period is, in fact, an unofficial "Long Vacation" term. The majority of the fellows of colleges are in residence, and, while no compulsion can be exercised upon the undergraduate, he is encouraged to "come up for the Long" if he can. For students in Medicine, Natural Sciences, Mechanical sciences, and Geography the Long Vacation courses are specially valuable. Further, all undergraduates are housed for the time in college and the conventional distinctions between "first year", "second year", and "third year" tend to disappear.

As the way in which the Long Vacation is spent may well depend upon financial considerations, this may be a convenient point at which to examine the cost of a Cambridge education. The table on page 87 is taken from *The Student's Handbook to the University and Colleges of Cambridge* for 1939 and summarises an undergraduate's expenses at that time. These figures do not include the additional fees for practical laboratory work payable

	Initial expenses			Expenses that recur annually		
	Lower scale	Average	Higher scale	Lower scale	Average	Higher scale
	£ s.	£ s.	£ s.	£ s.	£ s.	£ s.
Initial expenses						
Caution money	15 0¹	15 0¹	15 0¹	...	...	...
College admission fee.............	2 0	3 0	5 0	...	...	...
University matriculation fee...	5 0	5 0	5 0	...	...	...
Valuation of furniture	10 0	25 0	50 0	...	...	...
Repairs of rooms..................	3 0	4 0	6 0	...	...	...
Linen, china, etc.	5 0	8 0	15 0	...	...	...
Cap, gown and surplice.........	2 0	3 10	4 10	...	...	...
University fees						
Lecture fees	...	...	...	18 0²	18 0²	18 0²
Examinations	3 0	3 0	3 0	...	...	...
Degree fee (B.A.)	...	...	...	...	...	...
University capitation tax	...	...	...	5 5	5 5	5 5
Parliamentary Registration ...	...	...	...	...	...	...
College fees						
Tuition fee	...	...	...	21 0	27 0	27 0
Establishment charge.............	...	...	...	12 0	14 0	15 0
College dues	...	...	...	1 1	4 10	8 5
College degree fee	...	...	...	...	...	...
Board and lodging						
Rooms and service................	...	...	...	30 0	38 0	54 0
Dinner in Hall	...	...	...	20 0	24 0	27 0
Commons, etc. (including milk)	...	...	...	6 0	8 0	10 0
College kitchen	...	...	...	0 0	25 0	40 0
Coals and light	...	...	...	6 0	9 0	12 0
Laundress	...	...	...	3 0	6 0	9 0
Groceries, etc......................	...	...	...	15 0	20 0	30 0
				137 6	199 5	255 10
Personal expenses						
Books	...	...	...	8 0	10 0	15 0
Travelling	...	...	...	7 10	15 0	22 10
Tradesmen's bills (including tailor, etc.)	...	...	...	30 0	40 0	60 0
Clubs and Societies	1 1	3 3	5 5	5 5	9 0	15 0
	46 1	69 13	108 15	188 1	273 5	368 0
Possible additions						
Long Vacation.....................	...	...	...	0 0	20 0	35 0
Private tuition.....................	...	...	...	0 0	20 0	36 0

¹ The amount of this deposit, which is returned when the student leaves the university, varies between £15 and £30.
² Approximate figure for most literary subjects for honours students. For other students and subjects, it may be much increased.

by a student in Medicine, Natural Sciences, Engineering, Agriculture or Geography, and clearly it is the "occasional" and "additional" expenses which determine the final figure.[1] They are expenses which are for the most part within the undergraduate's own control: if his rooms are large rather than small, his clubs many rather than few, his means of transport a Bentley rather than a bicycle, his lunches expansive rather than frugal, his tastes horsey rather than bookish, the total amount of his annual expenditure will be correspondingly increased.

In general, it may be said that there is a wide divergence in undergraduate budgets. The poor scholar will adhere as closely as he can to the lower scale quoted in the table; at the other end of the scale, the well-to-do can find innumerable ways of exceeding his allowance; between them there is (or was before 1939) a large class which obtains a full measure of the proper enjoyment of university life on incomes of £300 a year or less.

In his second year the undergraduate may find himself saddled with minor responsibilities. It is the second year that normally provides university and college clubs and societies with secretaries, and the secretaryship, even of a small club, may be an experience of considerable value, bringing the holder of it into contact with members of varying age and temperament. By this time also the undergraduate is probably beginning to feel more at ease with some of the dons of his college and to realise that for the most part they do not wish to be regarded

[1] The annual expenses of a non-collegiate student are estimated at £160–200 according to the subject being studied.

as sublimated schoolmasters. If he is an enthusiastic motorist, he is free, under university regulations, to obtain leave from his tutor to keep a car or motor-bicycle, but college regulations vary: some follow the university rule; others allow cars only to third-year men; others forbid them to all undergraduates. Again, at the end of the academic year the undergraduate will probably be faced with a university examination; though it may well be the first part of a Tripos, it is often a final examination in the subject concerned, since the third year may be devoted to another subject.

As the second year provides the secretaries, so the third year provides the captains and presidents of clubs and societies. The captaincy, say of a college boat club, or the presidency of the Union Society may provide an undergraduate with administrative experience of real value and will certainly occupy a considerable portion of his time. Time, indeed, runs fast in the third year: the terms seem too short for all that must be crowded into them, and in one form or another there looms ahead the examination on which a degree, and the class of degree, depend. The lists of successful candidates, which are published about the middle of June, are divided into three classes and in some Triposes each class is divided into two divisions. Within the divisions, the order is alphabetical.[1] An undergraduate who is a scholar of his

[1] The Classical Tripos lists were arranged in order of merit until 1882; the Mathematical Tripos lists until 1909. With the abolition of this order, the titles of Senior Classic and Senior Wrangler (see p. 19) disappeared.

college will normally expect, or be expected, to be placed in one or other division of the first class and a "first" may be of real importance to his career. But a second or a third class does not signify failure. All those whose names appear in the Tripos list have earned an "honours" degree. Failure to reach the honours standard is frequently mitigated by an "allowance", in whole or in part, of an "ordinary" degree. The results of the examinations both of Triposes and of Ordinary Degree examinations are published on or before a Saturday in the middle of June, and the successful candidates are qualified, like their medieval predecessors, to become "commencing" bachelors. On the Saturday there is held in the Senate-House a Congregation at which there is a "general admission" of "poll" men to degrees. The following Sunday is still called Commencement Sunday and two days later, on Commencement Tuesday, there is another Congregation at which honours men are admitted to degrees. The ceremony is in some colleges preceded by a "degree breakfast" in the college hall. The Praelector presides and afterwards leads his candidates to the Senate-House. The candidates wear dark clothes, white ties, bands, with B.A. hoods ("of black stuff, part-lined with white fur, the tippet edged with white fur") over their undergraduate gowns. In groups of three or four they are presented by their Praelector to the Vice-Chancellor; the Praelector de-'clares, in Latin, that he knows the candidate to be fit, on grounds both of morals and of learning, for the Bachelor's degree; each candidate kneels in turn and over each the Vice-Chancellor pronounces the formula:

Auctoritate mihi commissa admitto te ad gradum Baccalaurei in Artibus in nomine Patris et Filii et Spiritus Sancti.

The candidate leaves the Senate-House a Commencing Bachelor.

In this sketch of some of the features of undergraduate life no reference has been made to the women's colleges. As has already been noted, the admission of women to full membership of the university was not approved until 1947. For most practical purposes, however, the life of a junior member of Girton or Newnham has for long been very similar *mutatis mutandis* to that of a male undergraduate. All university lectures, libraries and laboratories have for many years been open to them; they have sat for the same examinations as men and their names have appeared in the Tripos lists; they have been encouraged to engage in research. But they have not been matriculated members of the university and they have been admitted only to titles of degrees. Now, at length, the logical conclusion has been reached and from the beginning of the academical year 1948–49 Girton and Newnham are to be constituent colleges of the university.

¹ The total number of women students is limited, by Ordinance, to 500.

V

POSTGRADUATE

In every year about 1400 undergraduates are admitted to the degree of Bachelor of Arts in the University of Cambridge. What becomes of them? The majority leave Cambridge; a smaller number remain in residence as bachelors and continue their studies. This may be done with a variety of objects. The man who has been placed in the First Class of a Tripos may be looking towards an academic career. For such a man his college is generally glad to extend the period of the tenure of his scholarship, and he may elect to read for another Tripos; or he may be a candidate for one of the many scholarships or prizes offered by the university and designed to enable a student to undertake a year's research in some special branch of his subject; or he may officially become a "Research Student", that is, he may, with the approval of the Degree Committee of a Faculty and of the Board of Research Studies, become a candidate for a "research" degree to be obtained by means of a dissertation on a subject proposed by him and approved by the board. Such a candidate is placed under a supervisor in the university who directs his work; he may apply for the degree of Doctor of Philosophy (Ph.D.) [1] for which two or three years' work is required; for the degree of Master of Science (M.Sc.) or Master of Letters (M.Litt.) only one or two years' work is necessary.

A Bachelor of Arts who has hopes of a college fellowship is not required to obtain a "research" degree. The system of election to fellowships varies in different colleges: a few elect upon dissertations submitted by the candidates, but the majority elect without examination of any kind, and a promising scholar may well be elected at the end of his fourth year. There is indeed no uniform plan for the election of a fellow of a college: one fellow may be elected at the end of a year's private work; another after two or three years of advanced study at a foreign university; another in view of his suitability for a tutorship or other important college office; another after several years spent as a teacher either at Cambridge or elsewhere.

A certain proportion of Bachelors of Arts who remain in Cambridge with a view to advanced study may be elected to administrative or teaching posts in the university without obtaining fellowships; and the Laboratories and Museums as well as such institutions as the University Library and the University Press provide a number of openings of this kind.

It should be added that the status of "Research Student" is open to graduates of other universities, and

---

[1] A Ph.D. may be obtained in any subject. Its association with philosophy is purely nominal.

there is a considerable body of such students resident in Cambridge. Like the freshman coming from school, the Research Student must first be admitted to a college or as a non-collegiate student; he must secure approval of his proposed subject, must carry out his research under a supervisor, and must reside for the period prescribed for the degree which he seeks. A large number of such students are graduates of universities in the Dominions and in the United States, and at the present time there are about 250 students who are engaged in research under these conditions. There is no organised "postgraduate" school, but the subjects of research cover a wide field and vary from Sanskrit Plays to Poultry Nutrition, from Coptic to Internal Combustion Engines, and from Ancient Hydraulics to the Philosophy of Religion.

Apart from those bachelors who, after engaging in some form of research, obtain appointments in Cambridge, a considerable number reside for a fourth year with no intention or expectation of staying longer, but with a view to additional equipment for a career elsewhere. Candidates for the ministry of the Church of England or of the Free Churches may enter one of the theological training schools in Cambridge[1] without breaking their connection with their own colleges; candidates for the various Civil Service examinations have special courses provided for them; or, again, those

[1] Westcott House, Ridley Hall (Anglican); Westminster College (Presbyterian); Wesley House (Wesleyan); Cheshunt College (Congregational).

who intend to engage in some form of teaching may gain a real advantage by an additional year's study at Cambridge. Thus every college has its group of bachelors. Though they are technically still *in statu pupillari* and therefore subject to the jurisdiction of the Proctors, they have certain privileges in college and their expenses are slightly less than those of an undergraduate. They have their own table in the college hall and are free to take as much, or as little, part in social and athletic activities as they please. Between them and the undergraduates there is no kind of barrier, but the bachelor may well seize the opportunity to learn a little more about some university institutions than his scanty leisure as an undergraduate allowed him. The choice will depend upon temperament, but he may well improve his acquaintance with the University Library or the Fitzwilliam Museum, with the Laboratories or the Botanic Garden; he may discover that a University Sermon may be worth hearing or the fenland churches worth exploring; he may even study the history of his own college or the architecture of some others.

But for the majority, as has been said, Commencement Tuesday is the end of academic life. Many, of course, have made their choice of a career long before taking their degree, perhaps before coming into residence. The medical student goes off to a hospital; the legal student to a solicitor's office or to one of the Inns of Court; the candidate for Holy Orders to a theological college; others may go straight into business, to the staff of a school, to the office of a newspaper, to engineering

95

works, to an architect's office, or to a variety of other employments at home or abroad. In his third year an undergraduate may well have received valuable help and advice from his tutor regarding his career, and there also exists in Cambridge a University Appointments Board, an organisation which for the last thirty years has been of great value in securing suitable employment for members of the university. Undergraduates may register their names at the beginning of their third year, and a staff of secretaries acts as a link between the professions and industries on the one hand and the undergraduate, or graduate, on the other. Employers and directors of institutions both at home and abroad regularly inform the Appointments Board of vacancies and the board keeps in touch with its registered members long after they have gone down from Cambridge.

One privilege is acquired by all Bachelors of Arts—that of qualifying as Parliamentary Electors, for the University. By the Representation of the People Act of 1918, every Bachelor of Arts, not otherwise disqualified, has a vote for the University Representatives in Parliament, and the privilege extends to women who have been admitted to the title of the degree.

Whether resident or non-resident, the Bachelor of Arts may be admitted Master of Arts six years after the end of his first term of residence.[1] The resident bachelor naturally proceeds to the degree at the earliest oppor-

[1] Provided that two years have elapsed since he was admitted Bachelor of Arts.

tunity. There is no examination; certain fees are paid[1] and, as before, the candidate is presented to the Vice-Chancellor by the Praelector of his college. A resident Master of Arts engaged in teaching or administrative work in the university or in a college becomes, as has already been explained,[2] a member of the Regent House and so obtains a share in the day-to-day government of the university. If he is engaged in original work, he may in due course desire to proceed to a Doctor's degree. To do so he must " give proof of distinction by some original contribution to the advancement of Science or of Learning ",[3] that is, he must present some work of his own for consideration by a committee of the faculty concerned.

The successful candidate for a doctorate is presented for his degree by the head of the faculty and becomes entitled to wear a doctor's hood and gown. In place of the sober hood of the Master of Arts (of black corded silk lined with white silk) he wears a hood in which scarlet, combined with some other colour according to the degree conferred, predominates. He also wears a gown of a more elaborate pattern than that of a Master of Arts and on festal occasions wears a red gown.[4]

---

[1] The university fee is £3.   [2] See p. 53.

[3] The quotation is from the regulations for the Doctorates of Science and of Letters. A similar proof is demanded for other doctorates.

[4] There are, however, two exceptions: a Doctor of Music wears a gown of cream damask, lined with dark cherry satin; a Doctor of Philosophy wears a black gown with a facing of scarlet cloth.

In the calendar of the university certain days are "Scarlet Days": All Saints' Day, Christmas Day, Easter Day, Ascension Day, Whit Sunday, Trinity Sunday, Commencement Saturday and Tuesday, and the Sunday on which benefactors are commemorated in the University Church are officially days on which doctors wear their scarlet, and both the university and the individual colleges frequently request that scarlet may be worn on other ceremonial occasions.

A doctorate gives its holder certain formal privileges of seniority in the university, but does not affect his status either in the Regent House or in his college. A professor, or a master of a college, is often a Master of Arts and nothing more.

The non-resident Bachelor of Arts is as free to proceed to the degree of Master of Arts and to the higher degrees as the resident. Provided that he has kept his name on the college boards,[1] the non-resident Master of Arts becomes qualified to be placed on the Register of Members of the Senate and so is entitled to vote on certain Graces. Further, like the resident Master of Arts, he is entitled to borrow not more than ten books from the University Library. What he may value even more is his permanent membership of his college. Every few years he is invited, with his contemporaries, to a Commemoration dinner and in many other ways he is given the opportunity of keeping in touch with the

[1] In all but a few colleges, the names of B.A.'s are retained upon the college boards without fee.

98

college. He may in course of time enter his son as a candidate for admission and an association of a family with a particular college for several generations is not uncommon. If a non-resident Master of Arts is following an academic career or is engaged in research, he may well proceed at some time to a doctor's degree; if he becomes highly distinguished in the world of learning or in public affairs, he may be offered the highest honour his college can confer, an Honorary Fellowship.

But there are many other occasions on which a non-resident Master of Arts may revisit either the university or his college, or both. If he is in politics, he may be invited to speak at a Union Society debate; if he has a reputation as an oarsman, he may come up to coach a college boat for a few days; if he is in Holy Orders, he may be invited to preach either in the University Church or in his college chapel; if he is on the staff of a university or hospital or other learned institution, he may be appointed an examiner in some university examination; if he is in the world of art or of science or of letters, he may be asked to read a paper at a meeting of some university or college society; or he may simply be asked by a friend to spend a week-end in college. In these and a hundred other ways the non-resident may keep his association with Alma Mater in constant repair.

A Cambridge man has two loyalties—the one to his university, the other to his college. At different times one or other form of loyalty will predominate. On boat race day he is essentially a "Cambridge" man, even if he be in some remote corner of the earth—distance, indeed, will make his patriotism grow more fervid. On the other hand, when he returns to Cambridge, it is to his college that his heart will warm. After an absence of some years he may well find that many men and things have changed, but at the very entrance to his college he may rely on recognition and welcome. However long the interval, not only his name, but his staircase, his friends, his escapades will be remembered by the College Porter, who is indeed a symbol of the perpetuity of the ancient foundation whose threshold he guards.

INDEX

Dean of a college, 67
Demonstrators, 62
Denny Abbey, 5
Discipline, 84 f.
Divinity School, Old, 29
Doctorates, 53, 93, 97 f.
Doket, Andrew, 8
Downing College, 20, 49, 72;
site, 49

Edward II, 5
Edward III, 5, 43
Edward IV, 8
Elizabeth, Queen, 13, 15, 43
Elizabeth Woodville, 8
Ely, Bishops of, 5, 7
Emmanuel College, 14, 48, 72
Erasmus, 10, 35
Eton College, 7
Examination School, 50
Examinations, Development of,
10; for college scholarships,
72; for degrees, 77 ff.
Exhibitioners, 65 n.
Expenses, Undergraduate, 86 ff.
Extension Movement, University, 23
Extra-Mural Studies, Board of,
24, 35, 57

Faculties, 56 ff., 62
Farmer, Richard, 48
Fellows of colleges, 63 ff., 93;
honorary, 99
Fenner's, 82 f.
Finance, University, 26 f.
Financial Board, 55
Fisher, John, 9, 10
Fitzwilliam House, 25, 50, 72
Fitzwilliam Museum, 50 f., 57

General Board, 56
George I, 30
Gibbs, James, 18, 38

Girton College, 24, 26, 46
Glaisher, J. W. L., 51
God's House, 8, 10, 47
Gonville, Edmund, 6
Gonville and Caius College, 6,
41 f., 72
Gonville Hall, 6, 13
Graces, 14, 54 ff., 58 ff.
Gray, Thomas, 32
Great St Mary's Church, 3, 41
Greek, Teaching of, 10 ff.
Grumbold, Robert, 44
Grumbold, Thomas, 39

Henry III, 2
Henry VI, 7, 8, 37 f., 47
Henry VIII, 5, 11 ff., 42 f.
"High table", 64, 68
Honours Degree, 77 ff.
Hood (B.A.), 90; (M.A.), 97;
(Doctor's), 97
Hullyer, John, 13

Ignoramus, 15

James I, 15
Jesus College, 1, 8, 46, 72
John XXII, Pope, 5
Jowett, Joseph, 40 f.

King's College, 7, 8, 37 f., 72,
79 n.
King's Hall, 5, 13, 42

Laboratories, 49 f.
Latimer, Hugh, 11, 13
Lecturers (University), 62; (College), 68 f.
Legislation, University, 54, 59 f.
Library, University (old), 3,
29 f., 37, 38; (new), 27, 30,
39 f., 57, 93
"Little-Go", 73
Local Examinations, 23, 35, 57

Lodgings, 74 f.
Long Vacation, 86

Magdalene College, 12, 45, 65 n., 72
Mallory, George, 45
Margaret of Anjou, 8
Margaret, The Lady, 9, 10, 43, 47
Market Hill, 41
Marlay, C. B., 51
Marshal, University, 61
Martin V, Pope, 7
Mason, William, 33
Master of Arts, Degree of, 3, 53, 96 ff.
Master (of a college), 63 ff., 70
Mathematics, Rise of, 16 ff.
Matriculation, 52, 76
Maxwell, Clerk, 21 f.
May Week, 85
Meals, Undergraduate, 75
Medicine, Degrees in, 78
Mey, William, 12
Michaelhouse, 4, 5, 13, 42
Midsummer Common, 46
Mildmay, Sir Walter, 14
Milton, John, 15 n., 34, 43, 48
Morley, Lord, 30
Museums, Science, 49
Music, Degrees in, 78 f.

Nevile, Thomas, 43
Newnham College, 24, 26, 40
Newton, Isaac, 16, 43
Non-collegiate students, 25, 72
"Non placet", 59 f.
Non-Regents, 6, 13

Officers' Training Corps, 80
Optimes, Senior and Junior, 19
Orator, 61
Ordinances, 54, 57, 77 f.
Ordinary Degree, 77, 90

Oxford, Athletic contests against, 82 f.; University of, 2, 16, 64
Oxford and Cambridge Schools Examination Board, 23

Parker, Matthew, 12, 37
Parliament, University Representation in, 15, 96
Pembroke College, 5, 32 f., 63, 72
Pensionarii, 9
Pensions, 27
Pepys, Samuel, 45
Peterhouse, 4, 31, 51, 71
Pitt, William, 33
Pitt Press, 34
"Placet", 59 f.
Platonists, Cambridge, 16, 48
Poll Men, 19, 77, 90
Praelector, 68, 76, 90
Press, University, 34, 57, 93 (see also *Printing* and *Pitt Press*)
Previous Examination, 53, 72 f.
Printing, Introduction of, 10; charter for, 11, 34
Proctors, 7, 14, 59 ff., 84 f.
Professors, 12, 16, 19 f., 62

Quadrivium, 3, 8
Queens' College, 8, 35 f., 72

Readers, University, 62
Redman, John, 12
Reformation, 10 ff.
Regent House, 53, 97
Regents, 6, 13 f.
Registrary, 12, 55, 76
Religious tests, 20
Renaissance, 9 ff.
Reporter, University, 58
Research Students, 92 ff.
Research Studies, Board of, 57, 92
Ridley, Nicholas, 13
Ridley Hall, 40

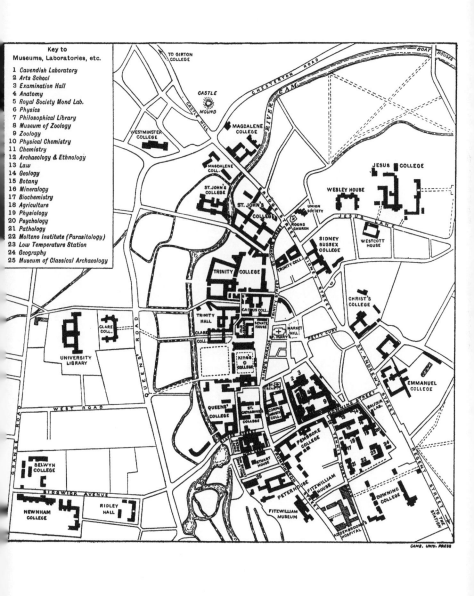

Key to
Museums, Laboratories, etc.

1 *Cavendish Laboratory*
2 *Arts School*
3 *Examination Hall*
4 *Anatomy*
5 *Royal Society Mond Lab.*
6 *Physics*
7 *Philosophical Library*
8 *Museum of Zoology*
9 *Zoology*
10 *Physical Chemistry*
11 *Chemistry*
12 *Archaeology & Ethnology*
13 *Law*
14 *Geology*
15 *Botany*
16 *Mineralogy*
17 *Biochemistry*
18 *Agriculture*
19 *Physiology*
20 *Psychology*
21 *Pathology*
22 *Molteno Institute (Parasitology)*
23 *Low Temperature Station*
24 *Geography*
25 *Museum of Classical Archaeology*

For EU product safety concerns, contact us at Calle de José Abascal, 56–1°, 28003 Madrid, Spain or eugpsr@cambridge.org.